WATSON & CO.'S
BEST AXE
HAND MADE
MADE EXPRESSLY FOR

AXE
HAND FORGED
BUCKFIELD FARMERS UNION
Buckfield, Maine

BEST AXE
HAND MADE

DIAMOND

ur Best
AXE
MANUFACTURED FOR
WEEKS & SONS
Meredith, N. H.

ENTRAL MAINE
AXE
Hand Made
roctor & Bowie Co.

Emerson & Steve

LUMBER
A
AND MADE

THE
VSEN SP
(Not Warrant
r money refund
best axe you eve
rice.
Manufactured by
ARSH & SONS CO.

FIRE AXE
WORKS AT OAKLAND, MAINE.
LIFE PROTECTOR
NORTH WAYNE TOOL CO.

THE LUMBERMAN'S PRIDE
WEDGE
MADE
Manufactured only by
EMERSON & STEVENS M
OAKLAND, ME.

OUR LIGHTNING CHOPPER
NO OTHER LIKE IT
COMBINED INLAID AN
OVERCOAT STEEL
STRONGEST WEL
LONGEST
WEAR
SEE THE STEEL
EATON
OVERCOAT STEEL
OVERCOAT STEEL
AND
RANTEED
OL CO. OAKLAND, M

THE GIANT
OKIT
XE
YNE TOOL CO.

The
CHOPPERS FAVORITE
AXE
Made of
HIGHEST GRADE
STEEL
JAQUITH HANDLE MILL · CLINTON, MAINE.

AX

C. M. BEAC
NEW MILFORD,

EX
HA
BES
BIT
AX
mpl
E
OOL CO.
ND, Maine.

HUNTER
WORKS AT OAKLAND, MAINE.
NORTH WAYNE TOOL CO.
HALLOWELL. MAINE.

IDEA

AND

ADE

OU
H

W. NOYES'
EASY CUT
AXE
Hand Made
H. W. NOYES, — Bristol, N

THE
PINE TREE
ALL HAMMERED
AXE
Manufactured only by
EMERSON & STEVENS MFG CO.

THE

S B
Made
KE

KEEN

THE HOTCHK

OUR BEST
AXE
HAND FO
F. A. DO
Williamsto

LOW PRIC
AXE
E GOOD
NOT GUA

STER'S FAVORITE
LL HAMMERED
AXE

M MANUFACTURING CO
ASTFORD, CONN.
OREST KING
AXE

C. P. Ste
Easy Cut
AXE

HAND MADE
CHARCOAL TEMPER
MANUFACTURED BY
NORTH WAYNE TOOL COMPANY.
HALLOWELL, MAINE.

G OF

TH
UT
X
m the

THE WOODS
HAND MADE
MADE EXPRESSLY FOR

American
AXE

American
AXE

Celebrating
THE TOOL
That Shaped
A CONTINENT

Brett McLeod

Storey Publishing

The mission of Storey Publishing is to serve our customers by
publishing practical information that encourages
personal independence in harmony with the environment.

Edited by Carleen Madigan
Art direction and book design by Alethea Morrison
Text production by Erin Dawson
Indexed by Nancy D. Wood

Cover photography by Mars Vilaubi

Interior photography credits
Mars Vilaubi, 11, 13, 14, 15, 16, 17, 18, 19, 20, 21, 22, 23, 24, 25 bottom, 26 top, 27, 28, 29, 46, 47, 52, 53, 54, 55, 56 right, 62, 63, 64 top, 65, 66, 67 left, 68, 69, 72, 74, 76, 77, 80 top, 81, 82, 83, 88, 89, 90 top, 91, 94, 95, 96, 97, 98, 99, 100, 101, 102, 103, 104, 105, 106, 107, 108, 109, 110, 111, 112, 113, 114, 115, 116, 117, 118, 119, 120, 121, 124 top, 125, 126, 127, 128, 129, 136 top, 137, 138, 139, 142, 143, 148, 149, 165, 189, 190, 191, 192

© HeshPhoto, Inc., 1, 2, 3, 5, 6, 8, 38, 40, 44 bottom, 45, 48, 49, 50, 51, 57, 80 bottom, 84, 86, 122, 124 bottom, 130, 131, 132, 133, 134, 136 bottom, 140, 141, 144, 145, 146, 147, 150, 152, 154, 155, 156, 157, 158, 159, 160, 161, 162, 163, 164, 166, 168, 171, 172, 175, 176, 177, 178, 179, 180, 181, 182, 183, 184, 185, 186, 187, 188

Additional interior photography by © Bettmann Archive/Getty Images, 90 bottom; © Bloomberg/Getty Images, 26 bottom; Courtesy of Brett McLeod, 73, 92, 93; © Buyenlarge/Getty Images, 71 top; © Dennis Rowe/Getty Images, 78, 79; © John Gruen, 67 right; © Keith Douglas/Alamy Stock Photo, 60; Courtesy of Library of Congress, Historical American Buildings Survey 56 left, 59, 70; Photo by Penn. State Dept. of Forestry 71 bottom; © madredus/stock .adobe.com: 61 top; © Photo 12/Alamy Stock Photo, 58; © Pictorial Press Ltd./Alamy Stock Photo, 64 bottom; © Sergey Shcherbakov/Alamy Stock Photo, 61 bottom; © Sunset Boulevard/Corbis/Getty Images, 25 top; © Universal History Archive/Getty Images, 44 top; © ZUMA Press, Inc./Alamy Stock Photo, 25 middle

Illustrations by © Megan Bishop: 30–37; C. W. Jefferys, excerpted from "Felling Axes" from *The Picture Gallery of Canadian History* by C. W. Jefferys (Ryerson Press, 1950): 43; © Jack Sobon: 67; © Michael Gellatly: 173

Storey books are available at special discounts when purchased in bulk for premiums and sales promotions as well as for fund-raising or educational use. Special editions or book excerpts can also be created to specification. For details, please call 800-827-8673, or send an email to sales@storey.com.

Storey Publishing
210 MASS MoCA Way
North Adams, MA 01247
storey.com

Printed in China by Toppan Leefung Printing Ltd.
10 9 8 7 6 5 4 3 2 1

Library of Congress Cataloging-in-Publication Data

Names: McLeod, Brett, author.
Title: American axe : the tool that shaped a continent / Brett McLeod.
Description: North Adams, MA : Storey Publishing, 2020. | Includes index. | Summary: "McLeod delves into the origins and usage of the axe, with profiles of vintage American axes, an exploration of log cabins, and a guide to collecting, restoring, and using a vintage axe, with overviews of axe games and axe throwing"— Provided by publisher.
Identifiers: LCCN 2020008610 (print) | LCCN 2020008611 (ebook) | ISBN 9781635861396 (hardcover) | ISBN 9781635861402 (ebook)
Subjects: LCSH: Axes—United States.
Classification: LCC TJ1201.A9 M35 2020 (print) | LCC TJ1201.A9 (ebook) | DDC 621.9/3—dc23
LC record available at https://lccn.loc.gov/2020008610
LC ebook record available at https://lccn.loc.gov/2020008611

CONTENTS

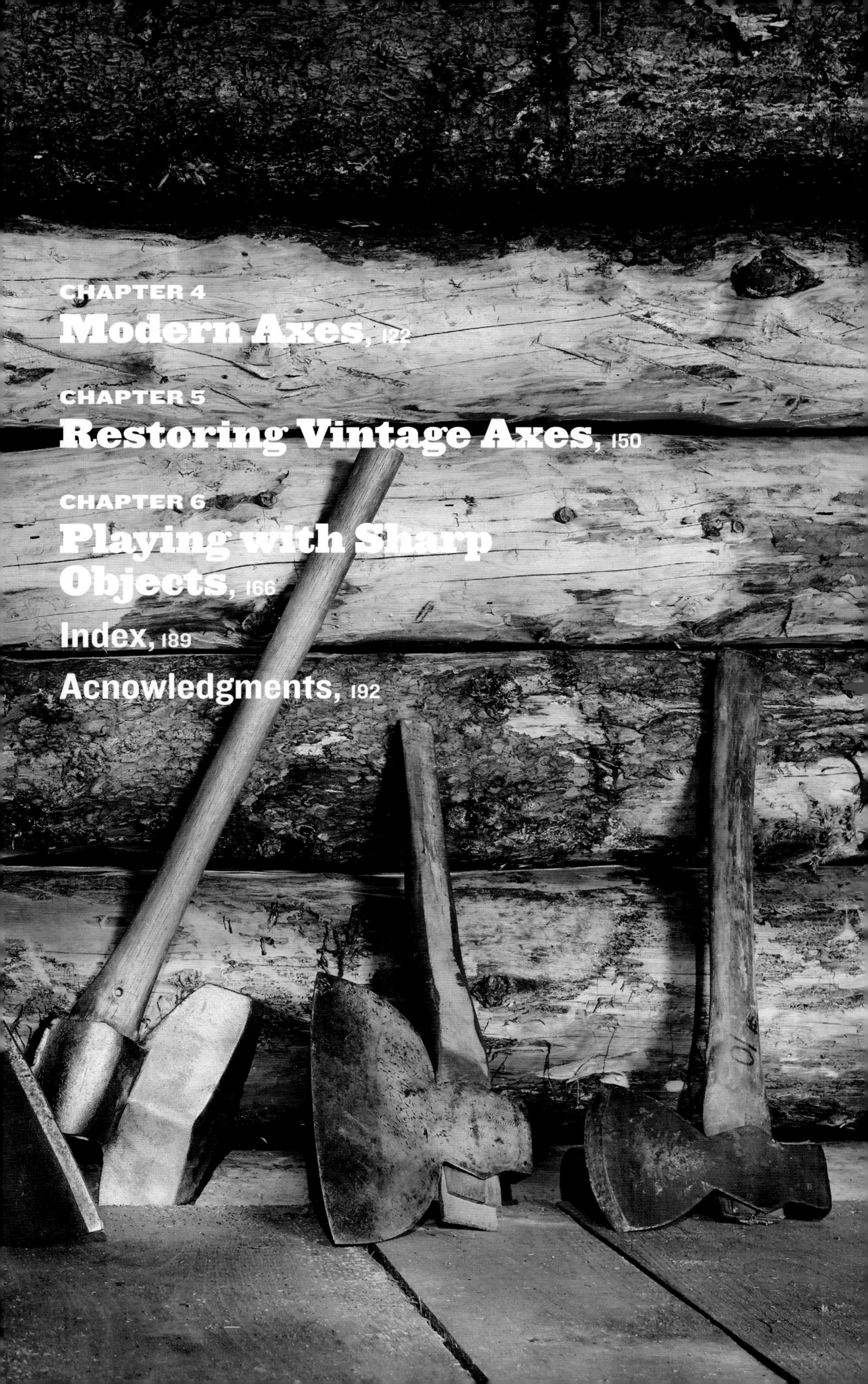

AXES
AND AMERICAN INGENUITY

The American landscape has been altered more by the axe than by any other tool. It is estimated that more than 300 million acres of timber were cut prior to the advent of the chainsaw in the mid-1920s. Although some of this wood was cut with crosscut saws in the late nineteenth and early twentieth centuries, most of it was felled, limbed, and bucked into log lengths entirely with an axe. Because the axe is such a simple tool — it's essentially a wedge with an edge — it was affordable to produce and acquire, enabling early settlers to carve out an agrarian existence from the forest. The axe was their ticket to a strong shelter, open ground for cultivation, a heat source, and even personal protection.

The first European-American axes were hand forged, but industrialization would be central to the development and distribution of the axe. Over the course of the late nineteenth and early twentieth centuries there were more than 1,000 different North American axe makers who engaged in a fiercely competitive market selling axes to lumberjacks, homesteaders, farmers, and foresters. What resulted from this lumberjack fever was a seemingly endless array of axe designs with impressive names such as The Woodslasher, Champion, Best Axe, Legitimus, Keen Kutter, Northern King, and the True Temper Perfect axe. Owners of these tools would proudly polish their axes to a mirror shine and argue the superiority of their chosen maker.

For some, the American axe has come to represent brute strength, the taming of nature, and even violence (Lizzie Borden comes to mind). But it's also a symbol of hard work, honesty, and simplicity. It's a tool that combines strength, utility, and aesthetic appeal — that's part of what makes them so fascinating and collectible.

Today, these vintage axes are being resurrected by both wood cutters and collectors alike. From a practical standpoint, vintage axes offer higher quality steel that holds a sharper edge than modern hardware store axes. For axe collectors like me, the lore associated with these tools is irresistible.

The slippery slope to obsessive axe collecting — what I call "axe-oholism" — always begins with pure, utilitarian intentions. Usually it's something like, "I need to clean up that old Boy Scout axe for this summer's camping trip," or, "I really should have a decent hatchet for splitting kindling." Over time, you'll discover that your love for the old axe you just restored runs so deep that you need another. If you can't admit that you need another, consider blaming the axe. Maybe the axe is lonely sitting in the corner of the garage without any companions? Or perhaps you've committed a cardinal sin and used a felling axe for splitting wood. (Time to scout out an old maul!) Consider yourself warned; you, too, may become an axe-oholic.

May your axe always have a keen edge!

Anatomy of an American Axe

Eye. The eye of the axe is the socket for the handle; it extends completely through the head.

Poll. Also sometimes referred to as the "butt" of the axe, and can be squared, beveled, or rounded. The poll is also the most common location for a stamped maker's mark.

Shoulder. Sometimes considered part of the poll, the shoulder's primary purpose on the American axe is to add weight, allowing for greater penetration of the axe.

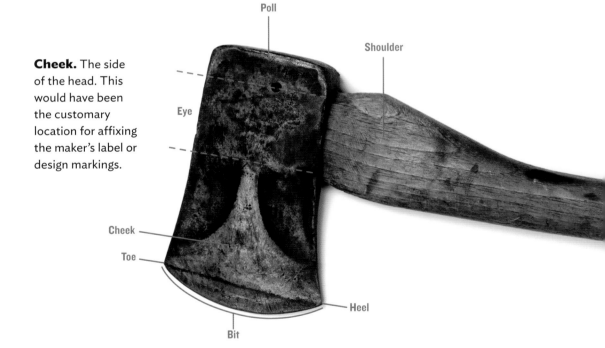

Poll

Shoulder

Cheek. The side of the head. This would have been the customary location for affixing the maker's label or design markings.

Eye

Cheek

Toe

Heel

Bit

Toe. This is the corner of the cutting edge farthest from the chopper. Axes that were misused for grubbing or chopping on the ground often feature an excessively worn toe.

Bit. The cutting edge of the axe which includes both the toe and the heel. The bit can either be inserted in the axe or wrapped around. Most early American axes were iron with a properly tempered steel bit that was forge welded.

Heel. The heel is the cutting corner closest to the chopper. This is the portion of the axe that should strike the wood first, and is considered the part of the axe that does the most work.

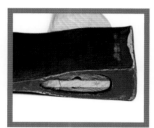

Bevels. The purpose of the bevel is to reduce the amount of contact area between the cheek of the axe and the wood. Many axes have bottom edge bevels; others have double or phantom bevels that run along both the top and bottom edges.

Ear or lug. This triangle or half-moon-shaped extension is found below the eye. The purpose of the lug is to add strength to the thinnest portion of the axe head.

Wedge. The wedge serves the purpose of holding the head tightly in the handle. Wedges may be constructed from wood (often poplar), steel, or aluminum.

Handle, or Haft

Doe's foot

Handle. Also known as a haft or helve, handles vary in length based on user preference, and may be curved or straight. Most American axes use hickory or ash due to their straight grain and flexibility.

Doe's foot. Also known as the "knob," or "deer foot," this feature helps maintain a firm grip.

How an Axe Is Made

TRADITIONALLY, AXES HAVE BEEN MADE by either casting or forging metal. Casting refers to heating steel (or another alloy) to the molten point and then pouring the molten metal into a form. This allowed for the mass production of socketed axes during the Bronze Age, though forging would become the dominant method in the subsequent Iron Age.

Forging is the process of hammering metal into its desired form while still in a solid state. The benefits of forging over casting is that forged axes have less surface and internal porosity, finer grain structure, higher tensile strength, and greater ductility. The reason for this is straightforward; when you melt metal for casting, the grain size is free to expand. When it cools back to a solid, the grain structure is coarser and more irregular, thereby decreasing its strength.

Prior to about 1850 most axes in America were hand forged, as early cast axes proved too brittle for the utilitarian demands of lumberjacks and pioneers. The strength of hand-forged axes was a function of hammering: as the steel is heated and folded, the metal laminates in sheets with finely aligned grain. Importantly, casting an actual axe head should be differentiated from the use of cast steel which is the starting material for modern forged axes.

The late 1800s brought the advent of the mechanical trip hammer which sped up the forging process and saved the blacksmith's arm. Both the trip hammer and forge are still in use today for small-scale axe production. However, most axes produced during the late nineteenth century to the present are drop forged — meaning that a mechanical hammer forces the steel into a die in the shape of the axe. Purists will still insist on the superiority of hand-forged axes, but undoubtedly the majority of timber in the world has been felled with a drop-forged axe.

Drop-forged axes begin with a single piece of cast steel, so that a separate bit doesn't need to be welded into the head. Instead, the bit is heat tempered to achieve the appropriate hardness; if the bit is too hard, it's prone to chipping/cracking. If it's too soft it will wear quickly and won't hold an edge. However, early hand-forged axes would use iron for most of the axe (much cheaper) and then hammer-weld a harder steel bit to the axe. This tried-and-true method is still used by blacksmiths who hand-forge axes.

The Making of a Modern Axe
Steps in the Process at the Brant & Cochran Forge

The Allagash Cruiser, a Maine wedge pattern camp axe, begins life as a 3.5-pound billet of American-made 1050 carbon steel, which resembles a giant hockey puck. ▶

The billet is then heated to 1,900°F in a gas forge before quickly heading to a hydraulic press, where it takes on its rectangular form. ▶

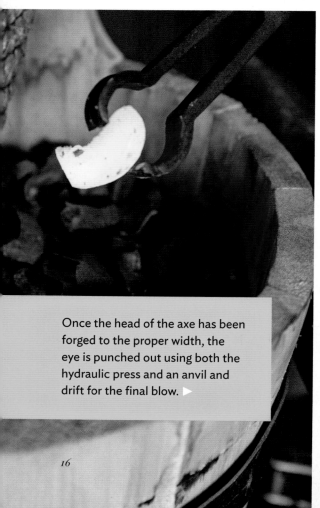

Once the head of the axe has been forged to the proper width, the eye is punched out using both the hydraulic press and an anvil and drift for the final blow. ▶

Drawing out the bit (fullering) in the hydraulic press, followed by lots of brute strength by the blacksmith at the anvil, transforms the head into a more recognizable shape. ▶

Once the head of the axe is shaped, the blacksmith uses calibration marks on the anvil to ensure the dimensions of the axe are within specifications. If an axe is under dimension, it heads to the scrap pile; if it's over dimension, it is ground on a belt sander to perfection.

In addition to the size and shape of the axe head, it is also essential that the eye of the axe is plumb with the bit. This is checked by sliding the head on a dummy handle, and then making sure that the wire on top falls directly in line with the center of the bit. ▶

The maker's mark, year, and temperer's initials are all hot stamped in the axe. In the early days of axe-making, it was essential to be able to trace an axe failure to the temperer, since brittle bits were the most common warrantee claim. ▶

The head is heat treated in a tempering oven at 1,500°F. ▶

The temper is then drawn back to a Rockwell hardness of 56, using the traditional salt bath method. The eye is then further softened to help absorb the shock of use. ▶

Finish grinding is done using a belt sander, and finally a whetstone. ▶

At this point, the head is ready to be hung on a traditional ash handle. A drawshave and its smaller cousin, the spokeshave, make quick work of sizing the eye of the handle. ▶

With the axe hung and wedged, the top is trimmed slightly "proud" extending just past the top of the axe head. ■

All in the Axe Family

AXES COME IN A VARIETY OF SHAPES and sizes to suit a range of tasks and users.

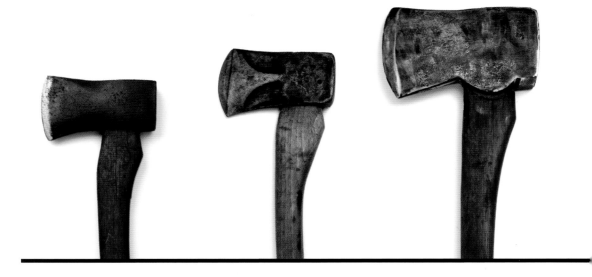

Hatchet. The smallest member of the axe family is the trusty hatchet. Its small size makes it easy to stow and carry, while the short handle affords control using just one hand. However, since the size of the axe is roughly proportional to the size of the job, you'll find the hatchet most appropriate for light chores like splitting kindling.

Boy's axe. A step up from the hatchet is a "boy's axe," which typically has a mid-length handle (about 28 inches) and a 2- to 2¾-pound head, making it ideal for a variety of chores. Its compact size makes it ideal for stowing in your camping pack, or behind the seat of your pickup.

Felling axe. A full-size felling axe has a long handle (31 to 36 inches) and a heavy head (3½ to 6 pounds). While originally designed to fell trees, the modern felling axe has a variety of uses around the home and in camp, despite having been replaced by the chainsaw.

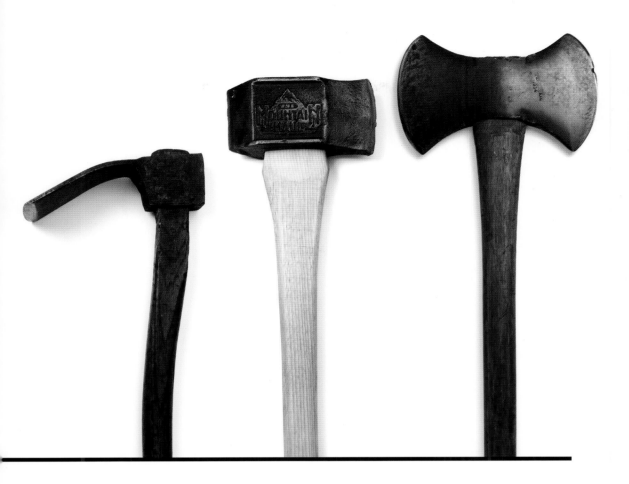

Adze. Dating back to the stone age, the adze is a cutting tool similar to an axe but with a cutting edge that is perpendicular to the handle, rather than parallel. Depending on the task, an adze can have either a short or long handle and the bit may be flat or curved. For example, coopers use a short-handled adze with a curved bit for making barrel staves, while a timber framer would use a long-handled adze with a wide, flat bit for further smoothing hewn timbers and floorboards.

Maul. A maul is half axe, half sledgehammer. Instead of cutting diagonally across the grain, a maul is designed to split the grain. Mauls range from 6 to 16 pounds in weight, have a blunt edge and a wide wedge to prevent sticking, and encourage splitting!

Throwing axe. The throwing axe has its origins in the logging camps, and was a way for lumberjacks to pass the time playing what is essentially a big dart game. A symmetrical 2–3-pound double-bit axe with long bits (up to 6 inches) and a 24- to 26-inch handle was considered ideal. The best throwing axe patterns included the bow tie, California reversible, and peeling axe. Today, axe makers produce bow-tie-pattern throwing axes that meet competition standards, including a pin through the axe head for safety.

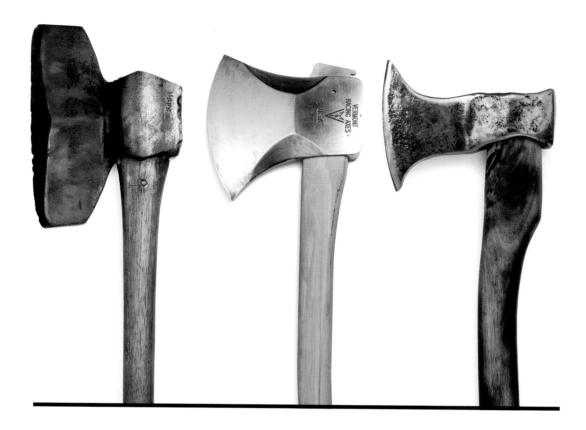

Broadaxe. While the term broadaxe is often used to refer to any wide-bitted axe, the hewing axe is certainly the most iconic broadaxe. Its design originated in Europe, with a true hewing broadaxe having only one side beveled. The flat side is kept parallel with the log, allowing the hewer to literally shave the log into a squared timber.

Racing axe. The racing axe shares about as much in common with a hardware-store felling axe as a NASCAR "stock car" with a Ford Focus. Racing axes are larger, use harder steel, and are truly razor sharp. Most of these axes weigh around 6 pounds and can have a cutting edge over 8 inches long. In capable hands during a wood-chopping competition, a racing axe can penetrate several inches with each blow.

Modified axe. The "mod" or modified axe refers to any stock axe that has been altered to improve the performance or design. The most common scenario for crafting a mod axe starts with an inexpensive, chunky foreign-made axe and then grinds away excessive steel to create beards, wings, and other bad-axe details. Many mod axes also sport intricate etchings and custom handles made of rare woods or custom laminates. No two mod axes are alike!

Beyond the Lumberjack: Axes for Other Uses

The lumberjack may be the primary master of the axe, but plenty of other professions have adapted the axe for specific tasks. Today, these axes have developed cult-like following within the professions where they were traditionally used.

Fire axe. The classic fire axe features a pick head pattern with a 4- to 5-inch spike that can be used for venting roofs, punching through steel siding, and prying open doors (or simply chopping through them; Jack Nicholson wielded a fire axe in the film *The Shining*). One of the most sought-after fire axes is the Seagrave Fire Axe manufactured by Collins especially for Seagrave, America's first fire apparatus company.

Pulaski axe. This innovative axe was created by U.S. Forest Service Ranger Ed Pulaski, after the 1910 Idaho Big Burn wildfire. It's a combination of a fire axe and an adze (or hoe), allowing firefighters to chop or dig simply by flipping it around, which makes it ideal for constructing fire lines. By the 1920s the Pulaski axe was standard U.S. Forest Service issue, and it continues to be used by wildland firefighters to this day.

Butcher's hatchet. Noted for its sharp bit (and sometimes a meat tenderizer on the poll), this hatchet was used for beheading fowl and breaking down the joints of larger livestock and game. While butchers may have owned one of these specialized hatchets, most homesteaders repurposed small hewing hatchets for butchering duties.

Fire axe

Pulaski axe

Butcher's hatchet

Crating hatchet. Prior to the advent of the cardboard box, most items were shipped in a wooden crate. This meant that both the wholesaler and the retailer would own a crating hatchet for packing/unpacking. These hatchets have a bit that could be used to split lath strips for the sides during crate construction, and then be used to help break the crate into kindling at the end of its serviceable life. The poll has a hammer head for closing the crates, as well as a claw and nail puller.

Tobacco hatchet. This cousin to the axe was originally made with a wide, thin blade with a sharp edge beveled on one side only and used for cutting the butt of tobacco plants. Variations of this tool were also used for cutting sugar cane, corn, and sorghum.

Tommy axe. A unique design made by True Temper, the Tommy Axe was targeted at outdoorsmen who wanted a compact and versatile tool. In addition to the tempered bit, it also has a heavy tempered poll that can be used as a hammer, and a claw that extends below the poll — ideal for pulling tent stakes.

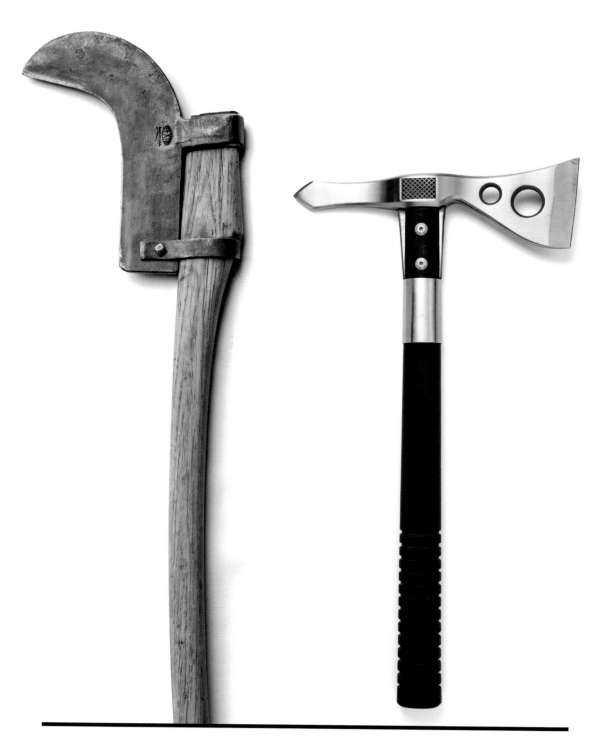

Brush axe. Also known as a brush hook, this tool was commonly used by land surveyors to clear branches for a line of sight, as well as to blaze boundary trees along property lines. A set of clamps attach the hook to a standard 36-inch felling axe handle.

Tactical hatchet. Developed for military and police use, this tool is employed for a variety of tasks including breaching operations, obstacle removal, and rescue. Modern tactical hatchets are often made of durable synthetic materials and can take extreme abuse.

Lath hatchet. Lath hatchets are closely related to shingle hatchets (page 63), but are generally smaller and lack gauge holes. Designed to cut and split lath strips for construction work and to drive nails, the lath hatchet was used in the era before plaster board became the standard.

Ice axe. This axe was used not to cut or harvest ice, but at the ice house to separate blocks of ice that were packed in sawdust until delivery. Because of its narrow bit, it's often confused with the mortising axe (page 67); the ice axe has a thinner profile to allow it to slide between blocks.

CHAPTER 1

ANCIENT AXES
THAT SPAWNED AN AMERICAN INDUSTRY

THE LINEAGE OF THE MODERN AMERICAN AXE IS ROOTED IN EUROPE. Early Europeans exploited metallurgy techniques to create both weapons and tools, and furthered the technology with developments such as tempering steel and sharpening techniques that kept a keen edge. The European immigrants who made their way to North America brought with them these unique trade skills. In the new land, they also found themselves free of government production controls; that allowed blacksmiths to become creative problem solvers in developing axes that were suitable for the formidable task of "taming the wilderness," as they saw it. With necessity driving innovation, and an ample supply of natural resources, it was a transformative time for the humble axe.

Stone, Bone, and Wood

How do you define what an axe is? And how long has this tool been around? If a sharp stone used in a chopping motion qualifies as an axe, then we have evidence that axes have been used for well over a million years, and probably closer to two million years. More refined stone axes with finely sharpened edges date back more than 300,000 years.

Although evidence of these early cutting and hacking tools — in the form of stone axe heads — is plentiful, it's likely that wood and bone axes were equally (if not more) prevalent, due to their ease of shaping and manipulation. Stone Age and later Neolithic petroglyphs suggest the use of femur bones to make a tool similar to a modern mattock or Pulaski axe. Stone hand axes were also used to skin animals, cut tendons, and break bones.

Archaeologists and anthropologists remain divided on the origins and date of the first hafted metal axe, mostly because it likely evolved in different geographic regions simultaneously. Stone axes persisted in some areas longer than others, particularly in regions where razor sharp obsidian and flint could be found. People living in places where copper and iron ore were more abundant and accessible naturally adopted those materials sooner. Scandinavia and parts of southern Europe, for example, were rich in copper and iron, so those regions developed a tradition of metal axe production, while central Europe served more as a trading partner than a producer.

Bison and horse jaw bones were commonly fashioned into hand axes by Native Americans. These axes were used for ceremonies, but were also sharpened for hunting and for battle.

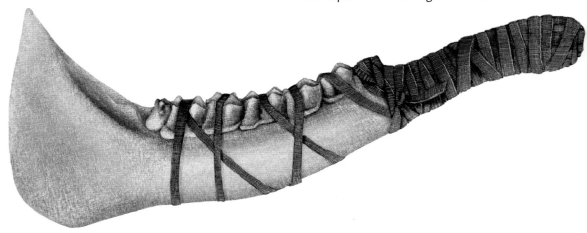

Ötzi and His Copper Axe

THE ARCHAEOLOGICAL DISCOVERY of "Ötzi the Iceman" (Europe's oldest mummy) in the Swiss Alps sheds light on the historically significant Copper Age that served as a transition time between the late Stone Age and the Bronze Age. Analysis shows that the copper axe Ötzi was carrying was actually made about 5,300 years ago in southern Tuscany — hundreds of miles between its point of origin and Ötzi's final resting spot. While the axe head is small and can fit in the palm of the hand, it was likely used to cut wood and for other utilitarian purposes.

The significance of this find is twofold. First, it suggests that Europeans were better-connected trade partners than first thought. Second, it serves as an early example of a forged axe that would evolve throughout the Bronze Age as a tool for both work and war.

The soft copper of Ötzi's axe could have been filed with a stone to sharpen the edge. The thin poll of the axe would have been lashed to a split handle with sinew.

The Bronze Age: Introducing Mass Production

IF YOU WERE IN THE MARKET for an axe during the Copper Age (around 5,000 BCE), you would have needed some serious bartering goods in the form of dozens of animal pelts, tin rings, and coils of woven rope, given the time and materials required to make a copper axe by hand. Copper axes, while superior to stone axes that could shatter, had several notable problems. One of the primary challenges to making an axe out of copper is that copper is exceptionally soft. In order to get a sharp edge, the maker would hammer or file the bit. The thinner the bit, the sharper the axe. However, a razor-thin edge is also very brittle and prone to chipping or folding. If the bit of the axe is too thick, the edge won't be fine enough to cut. Bronze, which is an alloy of copper (90 percent) and tin (10 percent), made for a more durable material when it appeared about 3,000 BCE.

As metallurgy knowledge increased, heading toward the Iron Age, axe makers and blade-smiths developed the ability to mass-produce tools and weapons, including the axe. Multiple casting molds were made out of sand, and then filled with the molten alloy, which melts at a relatively low temperature (1,742°F).

The use of casting also allowed for both solid and hollow axes. One popular form of hollow bronze axe was the socketed or celt axe which had a hollow poll that allowed for a handle to be inserted. These axes were mass-produced throughout Europe and had a head that was shaped much like a modern splitting maul. Interestingly, these bronze axes also served as currency — think of them as a more utilitarian gold bar!

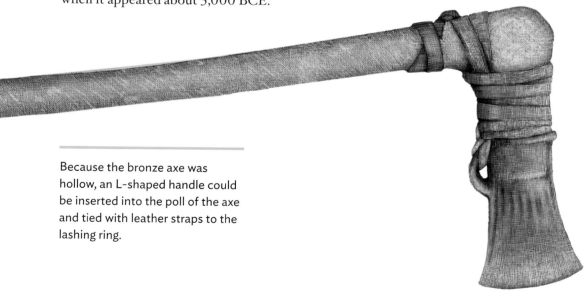

Because the bronze axe was hollow, an L-shaped handle could be inserted into the poll of the axe and tied with leather straps to the lashing ring.

Iron Age Axes and Agriculture

HISTORIANS SUSPECT THAT IRON was accidentally discovered when ore was tossed in a fire and cooled into twisted metal; the resulting material ushered in the Iron Age. In fact, there were several Iron Ages at different points in time, in many regions of the world (though not in North America). These periods are normally associated with innovation, but during the early Iron Age in northern Europe (about 2,500 years ago) many of the axes were simply reproductions of the earlier bronze designs. However, as blacksmithing skills developed, certain features were accepted as the new standard.

These included an eye for the handle that was parallel to the bit (instead of inserted in a parallel socket), and a wider bit capable of cutting more with each stroke.

The axe represented an important transition point in both tool development and land use during the Iron Age. The new, more efficient axe allowed for more land to be cleared, which necessitated the development of new iron cultivation and cutting tools including hoes, scythes, and pruning hooks. Collectively, these tools increased production and encouraged the clearing of land and expansion of agriculture.

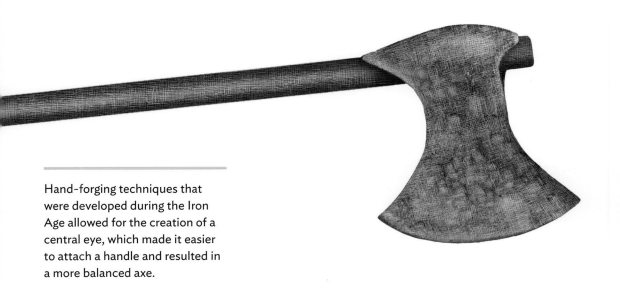

Hand-forging techniques that were developed during the Iron Age allowed for the creation of a central eye, which made it easier to attach a handle and resulted in a more balanced axe.

Axes for War

THE EXPANSION OF AGRICULTURE throughout Europe made arable land more valuable. With this came land grabs and inevitably war. Once again, the axe was at the forefront, this time as a weapon. The earliest battle axes were work axes that were modified with longer handles, offering a greater reach in battle.

In addition to long-handled battle axes, the end of the Iron Age in Europe also included the use of throwing axes. The Germanic Franks have a well-documented history of a short-handled, large-headed throwing axe used by nomadic warriors for hunting and in battle. It's likely that most of its battle use was for close combat, with the throwing capabilities of the axe reserved for the direst of situations since the warrior would be giving up his weapon. Testing of Frankish reproduction axes shows that it was calibrated to rotate once every 4 meters, making it very similar in calibration to modern throwing tomahawks that are thrown from a distance of 13 feet or 3.96 meters.

The refinement of war axes was the work of the Vikings. These Scandinavian axes bore the benefit of higher-quality steel (as opposed to unrefined iron) and quality craftsmanship. Although Hollywood would have you believe that these axes sported large double bits, there is no evidence that the Vikings ever had double-bitted battle axes. In the early Viking Age (first century CE) most of the axes featured a small (3- to 6-inch) single bit, while by the tenth century the Viking axes had a curved cutting bit 9 to 18 inches in width. The axes were sometimes decorated with inlays of other metals and engravings. The long, hooked heel of the axe allowed it to be used for climbing — presumably a benefit when trying to overtake fortress walls.

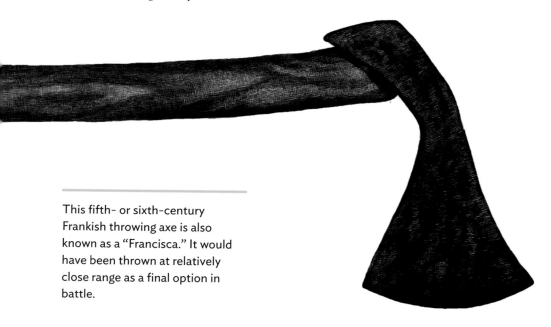

This fifth- or sixth-century Frankish throwing axe is also known as a "Francisca." It would have been thrown at relatively close range as a final option in battle.

NEAR RIGHT: This battle axe, found in Northern Ireland, was forged from a single piece of iron. The long handle made it a formidable challenger to the sword.

FAR RIGHT: The long, hooked heel of this Viking battle axe was key in overtaking fortress walls.

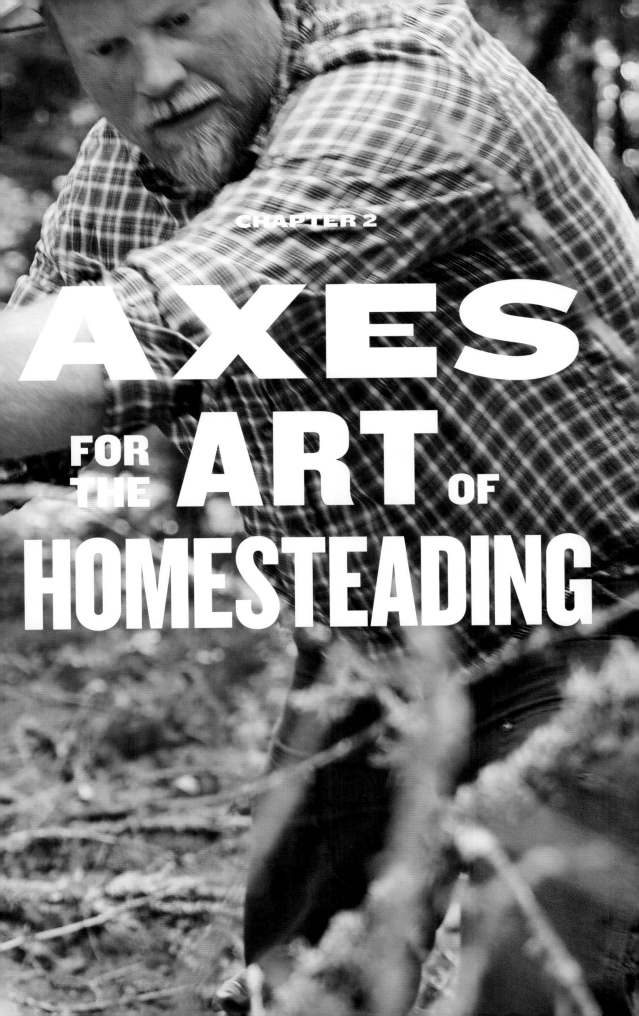

CHAPTER 2

AXES

FOR THE ART OF

HOMESTEADING

I T COULD BE ARGUED THAT NO TOOL HAS CHANGED THE AMERICAN LANDSCAPE MORE THAN THE AXE; the landscape also changed the tool. The Puritans brought farm axes from England that weren't big enough for felling the large timber in North America; their axes were lighter and needed modification to make them more efficient in their new setting. Blacksmiths wasted no time modifying the axes by adding poll weights, improving tempering so that axes held a keener edge, and developing specialized axes based on tree species, local preference, and the task at hand. By 1900, European settlers had managed to clear nearly 500,000,000 acres of forestland with the axe.

The European Axe Comes to North America

When Captain John Smith arrived in Jamestown, Virginia, in 1607 he was surprised to see that a hatchet known as the "trade axe" or tomahawk was a well-established form of currency. These early axes were French and Portuguese in origin, and were valued by the Native Americans as a versatile tool and symbol of heraldry. Driving the trade axe barter system was an insatiable appetite for furs in Europe, driven largely by French, Portuguese, and later Russian traders. However, the European axes would quickly morph into a distinctly American tool, as demanded by the rugged and wild landscape of North America.

When European settlers arrived in the forests of eastern North America, they quickly discovered that the smaller, lighter-weight European axes they had brought with them — which they had used on small-diameter coppiced trees back home — weren't up to the task of felling large-diameter timber that was better measured in feet than inches.

These early settlers made two modifications that resulted in the modern felling axe:

A heavier poll. First, the settlers added substantial weight to the poll of the axe. This additional weight meant that the woodsman didn't have to swing as hard and could instead let the weight of the axe do the work. More weight behind the handle also meant better balance, which made for truer swings.

A shorter bit. The settlers also shortened the bit (the cutting edge). Early European axes had a wide cutting edge, which made for an effective battle weapon but didn't allow for concentrated penetration when it came to chopping wood.

By the late eighteenth century, felling axes began developing regional identities as blacksmiths and lumberjacks named their axes after the places they were made; Connecticut, Michigan, Maine, and Pennsylvania became popular patterns. As they replaced the blacksmith, modern forges began to produce dozens of patterns for different uses and enough pattern choices to satisfy lumberjacks from coast to coast.

Noted Canadian historical illustrator and landscape painter C. W. Jefferys recognized the significance of the axe in shaping the North American landscape and documented the evolution of the axe in great detail.

FELLING AXES

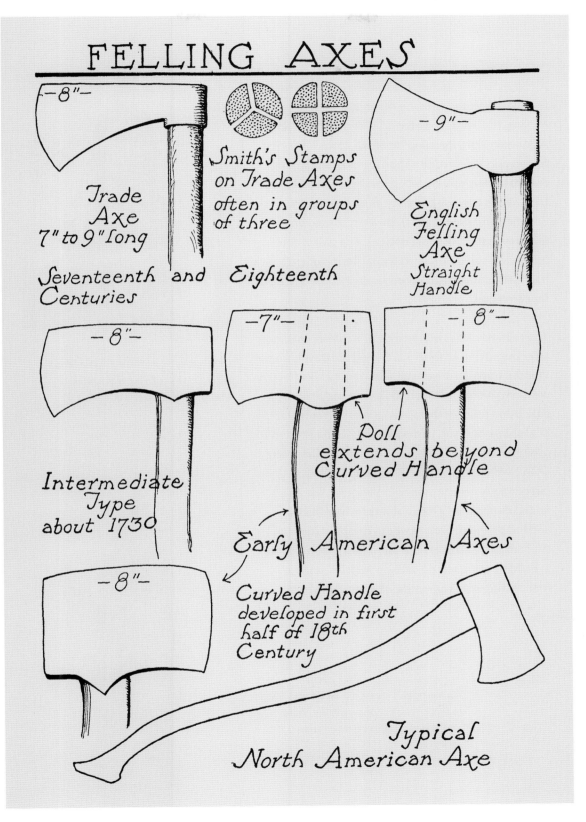

—8"—

Trade
Axe
7" to 9" long

Smith's Stamps
on Trade Axes
often in groups
of three

—9"—

English
Felling
Axe
Straight
Handle

Seventeenth and Eighteenth Centuries

—8"—

Intermediate
Type
about 1730

—7"—

—8"—

Poll
extends beyond
Curved Handle

Early American Axes

Curved Handle
developed in first
half of 18th
Century

—8"—

Typical
North American Axe

Tomahawks, Past and Present

A cousin to the hatchet, the tomahawk is believed to have originated with the Algonquin and Iroquois Indians; the word "tomahawk" is derived from an Algonquin word meaning "to strike down." The first tomahawks were made of bone, stone, and wood. French traders quickly recognized the value of metal tomahawks as trade currency; they specifically designed and produced "trade axes," based on the features that tribes most desired. The poll of the tomahawk could be spiked for battle, include a hammer for utilitarian purposes, or incorporate a pipe for ceremony.

The tomahawk has played a central role in wars, even after the advent of firearms. During the Revolutionary War the tomahawk was still seen as a highly effective weapon, given how long it took to reload a flintlock gun. During the Vietnam War, a World War II veteran of Mohawk descent, named Peter LaGana, started a business called the American Tomahawk Company (ATC) which shipped tactical war tomahawks directly to American troops in Vietnam. The ATC folded during the 1970s, but was revived in 2001 and has provided tomahawks to troops in Iraq and Afghanistan who use them for breaking down doors in building searches, de-arming vehicles, and for friendly throwing competitions around the base.

Chief Low Dog, of the Oglala Sioux tribe, poses with a ceremonial tomahawk, circa 1880.

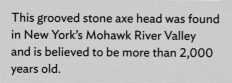

This grooved stone axe head was found in New York's Mohawk River Valley and is believed to be more than 2,000 years old.

This British trade tomahawk dates to the 1770s. Ironically, the Oneida Indians, who sided with the colonists during the Revolutionary War, used it in battle against the British.

This brass trade tomahawk dates to the French and Indian Wars, and was used both for ceremonial and utilitarian purposes. Note the functional pipe, which was hand drilled the length of the handle.

Building Shelter and Girdling Trees

Upon its entry to the "New World," the axe wasn't the tool of the lumberjack; it was the tool of the pioneer, a means of providing shelter and fuel. The American felling axe allowed homesteaders to clear land, build and heat their cabins, fence their livestock, and cook their food. With an axe, a basic cabin could be constructed in a week out of pole-sized timber. The notches of these early cabins were shallow and crude; the spaces between the logs were chinked with clay, plaster, oakum, moss, or anything that would reduce the draft and help keep the heat. The head of an axe was used to push the material to the center of the logs where it's tightest, to help close the gap.

Once the cabin was established, the axe was put to use girdling trees. By using the axe to scribe a ring around the tree, nutrients were cut off from the canopy, leaving a standing dead tree. This standing firewood was an important part of how the settlers kept warm in the winter, but on a grander scale allowed for massive burning of dead and dry forests that could then be converted to agricultural lands.

The punishing demands that were put on an axe also included abuse. Once the land was cleared, stumps still remained, which needed to be "grubbed out." While grub hoes appear to have co-evolved with the axe, many axes were used for grubbing stumps, which would lead to excessive wear on the toe of the axe from striking rocks and soil.

RIGHT: Early felling axes were formed by folding a single piece of iron. This resulted in an axe with a thin poll that wasn't really up to the task of heavy chopping.

This early axe was used for "grubbing stumps" as indicated by its worn toe.

Tree Felling, 1800s Style

Tree felling through the mid-1800s was done with just an axe. The woodsman would chop out a front notch in the direction he wanted the tree to fall, followed by a back cut. ▶

Using a series of 45-degree-angle swings, the woodsman would cut halfway through the tree before moving to the back cut. Chopping at an angle works with the grain, making it easier to remove the wood in large slabs. ▶

The woodsman would make the back cut identical to the face, leaving an equal amount of hinge wood on each side. Rather than chop through the hinge, the woodsman would let gravity do the rest of the work. ▶

As the tree began to fall, the woodsman would step back at least 12 feet, 45 degrees from the back cut. Once it was down, he would look up for other branches (known as "widow-makers") that may have been knocked loose in the felling process. ■

Squaring Timbers with a Broadaxe

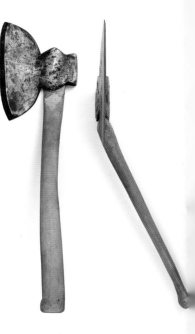

ALTHOUGH THE POOREST OF PIONEERS would have made do with a single-bit general-purpose axe, those of greater means might have also owned a broadaxe, which enabled them to slab off the rounded edges of the log and create square timbers — a process known as "hewing." Being able to take a round, tapered, and curved log and convert it to a cant (a four-sided timber) allowed for European building techniques to be incorporated in the New World.

Unlike the felling axe, the broadaxe remained relatively unchanged after its arrival in the New World. The broadaxe is easily recognized by its wide bit, but a true broadaxe is defined by one completely flat side and one beveled side. This allowed the axe to be used like a large chisel to shave away the curvature of a log. Most broadaxes carry a single-bevel bit that's filed to a razor-sharp edge.

To give the hewer control, broadaxes typically had a short handle — no longer than 24 inches. In order to protect the hewer's knuckles, an offset (curved) handle was used on the broadaxe. These handles were constructed using one of three methods. Axe makers in the early eighteenth and early nineteenth centuries often took standard handle stock and buried it in horse manure for weeks or months. The theory is that the fibers of wood absorb the ammonia from the manure and make the handle more flexible, so that it can then be clamped and dried at the desired angle. The second method involved using a curved branch or root with the desired offset, then using a drawshave to shape the handle. The final method is steam-bending, which is most successfully done with handles made of white ash.

The width of the broadaxe bit determined the spacing between the hewing notches. A larger, wider-bit hewing axe was more efficient, but it could weigh upwards of seven pounds.

The Sleeper Axe

As with other types of axes, the broadaxe evolved for other specialized uses beyond barn and home construction. The railroad tie axe (also known as a tie-hacker or sleeper axe) retained a common broadaxe pattern, but had a straight handle, a centered eye, and was beveled on both sides so that you could both fell a tree and hew a log with the same axe. Usually the ties (sleepers) were harvested in an area adjacent to the railroad tracks to minimize transportation distances. The number of ties needed was generally around 2,800 ties per mile.

As railroads expanded throughout the Northeast in the nineteenth century, demand for tie-hackers and sleeper axes increased. Nearly every Maine axe manufacturer had their own line of sleeper axes, including the 4.5-pound Peavey Little Giant Sleeper Axe.

The Adze

IF THE HEWN TIMBERS were for a barn, they were usually left rough. If the timbers were to be used in a house, they could be further refined using an adze. The adze looks a bit like a hoe, with a long, square-headed handle and straight cutting edge that's beveled toward the handle. By standing atop the hewn log and swinging the adze toward himself, a homebuilder could slice paper-thin sheets of wood that left the timber (or in many cases, the floorboards) perfectly smooth. It's worth mentioning that the square eye of the adze is intentional. Since the head is held on only by the force of the swing, the handle can be removed for sharpening, a task that would be nearly impossible with the handle fixed in place.

TOP AND RIGHT: Axes were used to do the rough work, but adzes were capable of smoothing surfaces as flat as sawn wood. Note the character marks on this adze-hewed bench.

LEFT: This log church, built in 1843, is constructed from hewn oak logs that have been adzed.

Specialized Axes for Cabin Building

THE NOTION THAT A LOG HOME could be built with the aid of a single tool has long captivated the minds of determined pioneers and dreamers alike. The earliest cabins of North America were constructed using a single axe for felling, bucking, peeling, notching, splitting, and even chinking. To own more than a single axe prior to the mid-nineteenth century would have been viewed by many as a luxury. However, the mid-1800s saw major technology and efficiency advances in mining, metallurgy, and manufacturing that drove down the prices of axes and created a space in the marketplace for specialized axes, hatchets, adzes, draw-shaves, and associated round wood tools.

The Felling Axe

Most felling axes weigh between 3½ and 6 pounds, and have a 31- to 36-inch-long handle and a 5-inch bit. These were the workhorses of the homestead, which were commonly used for chopping, splitting, pounding, and hewing, despite their intended purpose for felling and bucking into manageable lengths. Many log cabins were built entirely with the felling axe. Once the tree was felled and bucked into logs, the axe's master could hone the edge of the axe, grip the poll, and use it as a draw-shave to peel the log. Technique also played a major role in increasing the versatility of the felling axe. For example, by moving your hands closer to head of the axe ("choking up") the chopper has more control. This allowed the heavy felling axe to be used for other tasks, including intricate notch work.

However, as wealth increased, so did the toolbox of the log-smith, contributing to finer construction and greater efficiency. This spurred the development of axes in various sizes and configurations, as well as specialized tools for the log-smith.

LEFT: The axe was part of Abraham Lincoln's political narrative, as was his rustic upbringing on the frontier. When he ran for president in 1860, he became known as the "rail-splitter" candidate; his party marched at a rally carrying a banner lashed to two hand-split fence rails, purportedly made by Abe himself.

A Boy's Axe for Limbing

These were scaled-down versions of the larger felling axes, and are also referred to as camp axes, or cruisers. Typically between 2 and 2¾ pounds, these smaller axes were hung on 24- to 28-inch handles. As the name implies, they were traditionally made for young boys learning to swing an axe, but they could be used in a number of different applications. Their light weight made them ideal for limbing-out thick conifers with efficiency. Often, the boys would accompany the men into the woods, following behind the felling crews to limb out the timbers with their smaller axes.

Hewing Axe

Before the advent of the sawmill, if you wanted to make a cant, plank, or fireplace mantle for your cabin, you would use an axe. Hewing a log is labor-intensive, but the result is a material that's square and easy to build with. Accounts from the nineteenth century document that people spent weeks hewing dovetail cants, but just a day or two erecting the entire structure. Hewing is more akin to shaving than chopping, since thin layers of the log are sliced away perpendicular to the grain. A good, versatile hewing axe has a single-bevel 8- to 11-inch bit, and weighs in at around 5 to 7 pounds. The handle should bend left for right-handed hewers, and right for left-handed hewers; this prevents scuffing your knuckles on the log.

BELOW: This cabin, built in 1848, was constructed using adze-planed logs and dovetail corners.

Axe-Made Notches

The importance of good notch work when building a cabin cannot be overstated — notches tie the corners of the building together and, if made correctly, create a weatherproof shelter. While some notches could be entirely carved with an axe, the use of an adze made for tighter, cleaner notches. Like axe patterns, the notches used for log cabins often reflected their place of origin. The traditional saddle notch originated in Scandinavia and followed immigrants to the northern United States and Canada.

THE SADDLE NOTCH. To make a saddle notch, homebuilders used a log scribe to transfer the shape of the bottom log to the top log. The log on top always received the notch, since notching the bottom log would have created a pocket for moisture to collect and would have rotted the log prematurely. Once scribed, the felling axe was used to make a V-notch. As the builder approached the scribe line, he would have swapped the felling axe for a smaller boy's axe to allow for more control. Within a quarter inch of the scribe line, he would have switched to a hand adze and carefully chiseled his way down to the scribe line.

THE DOVETAIL NOTCH. In the mid-Atlantic and Appalachian regions, dovetail notches were common on cabins made of square timbers. To construct a dovetail notch, trapezoidal shapes were cut into logs to allow them to "interlock" together. Early Appalachian cabins used dovetail notches that were entirely constructed with an axe. Later notches appear to use a combination of axes, adzes, chisels, and saws. Using this method, the logs were often squared on all four sides by hewing. Instead of using a log scribe, a jig was used to mark the angles and proper depth of cut.

THE SWEDISH COPE. This is a variation of the traditional saddle notch — one that eliminated the need for chinking by scribing the contour of the bottom log along the entire length of the top log and then carving a groove with an axe and adze to mirror the contour. This was considered by many to be the finest method of log construction, but could take two or three times as long to construct, compared to a cabin made with saddle notches and chinking.

The Broad Hatchet and Shingle Hatchet

THE TRADITIONAL LOG CABIN roofing system consisted of hand-split shakes, with rot-resistant cedar being the wood of choice. Until the advent of the shingle mill in the late nineteenth century, shakes were made by hand using either a froe or an axe. The second method of making shakes consisted of using a small or broad hatchet to split the shake. The broad bit and single bevel worked like a chisel, slicing off shakes in line with the grain. A wooden mallet or club was sometimes used to help the hatchet through the wood.

The shingle hatchet (also called a roofing hatchet) differed from the broad hatchet in that it wasn't for making shakes, but for installing them. The narrow bit was for splitting shingles/shakes to the proper width, while the poll was for driving nails. Shingle hatchets also commonly had a nail puller built in, and some included an adjustable depth gauge allowing for uniform placement of the shingle row.

The broad hatchet (top) was used for making roof shingles; the shingle hatchet (right) was used for installing them.

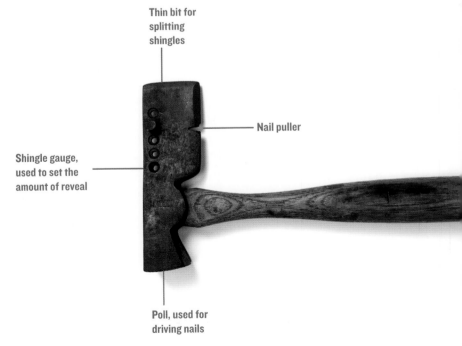

Thin bit for splitting shingles

Nail puller

Shingle gauge, used to set the amount of reveal

Poll, used for driving nails

Carpenter's Hatchet

A COUSIN TO THE SHINGLE HATCHET is the carpenter's hatchet (a.k.a. the half-hatchet), which one could consider the Swiss Army knife of the axe world. The bit on a carpenter's axe is wider than that of a traditional shingle hatchet, allowing it to be used for light hewing and evening of wood surfaces. The poll of the axe includes a hammer head stout enough to handle most hammering tasks. The lower edge of the beard includes a nail puller as well. In the 1800s, the utility of a carpenter's axe meant that a person could literally go from tree to furniture with a single tool.

Hatchets, Historically Misused

Although the axe was the favored tool of Honest Abe, it was also the chosen implement of those with more nefarious intentions. Because axes and hatchets were present in virtually every home, farm, and store in America through the mid-twentieth century, they served as an accessible weapon in times of rage. While ultimately acquitted of murder, Lizzie Borden was accused of using a carpenter's hatchet (with poll hammer and nail puller) to kill her father and stepmother in 1892. Four other axes were found in the basement of the Bordens' home, but it was the carpenter's hatchet that showed signs of tampering, with a broken handle and ashes sprinkled on the head, as if to suggest that it had innocently been collecting dust. Although detectives couldn't find any blood or human hair on the hatchet, they did find animal hair, suggesting that this hatchet could have been used for animal butchering.

The carpenter's hatchet is one of the few axes where the poll is intentionally designed for hammering. The poll is tempered to be softer than most axe polls and the sides of the eye are thicker for added strength.

The Mortising Axe

THE ONE SHORTCOMING OF THE CARPENTER'S AXE is that while it was incredibly versatile, the wide-bearded bit prevented the axe from being effective for chopping deep pockets or mortises. The mortising axe, with its long head and narrow bit, was specifically designed for hewing sills and notches in joints. Unlike a larger axe, the mortising axe or hatchet was meant for controlled, precision work. The mortising axe was helpful to early craftsmen because it allowed for the construction of strong joints that could be pegged together without the aid of expensive iron hardware.

ABOVE AND LEFT: The narrow bit of a mortising axe allows for deep, precise box cuts.

RIGHT: Timber framing relies on precise, tight joints instead of metal fasteners. The mortising axe was also used in the late eighteenth century for the mortises in post and rail fences.

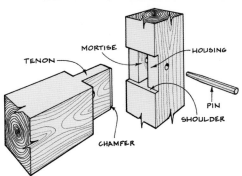

This axe was made for the Marshall Wells Hardware Company of Duluth, Minnesota. The embossing tells us it dates from between 1892 and 1915. This was considered a premium axe.

The Double-Bit Axe

A VARIATION OF THE SINGLE-BIT FELLING AXE was the double-bit axe, sometimes referred to as a "reversible." These axes first appeared in Pennsylvania between 1840 and 1850 and were commonly used in the Northeast by the 1860s. The debate continues as to whether a single-bit or double-bit axe is superior. Single-bit aficionados point to the fact that this axe benefits from a heavy poll, which allows the axe to penetrate deep into the wood.

Those who prefer the double-bit axe point to its utilitarian benefit: one bit can be kept stoutly sharpened for cutting knots and dirty wood, while the other can be finely honed for cutting clear and clean wood. Although this explanation appears straightforward, there are a variety of underlying reasons why the double-bit axe became so popular. First, consider the time frame in which it appeared; the 1840s represented a time of mass immigration to the United States. Although a generation earlier an immigrant would certainly expect to be pioneering, the antebellum period brought greater specialization of work, spurred on by increasing demand for virtually everything. This meant that the axe was no longer simply a multiuse tool of the homestead; it became a specialized tool for the industrial lumberjack. These lumberjacks were paid based on production, so having two bits (with one reserved for the dirty work) meant that less time was spent sharpening and more time was spent chopping. Additionally, new forging techniques made producing double-bit axes more economical, as hand-forging a double-bit axe was time-consuming and expensive.

The double-bit axe was popular because it combined two tools in one. One side would be dedicated to the dirty work of grubbing stumps and bucking muddy logs, while the "clean side" of the axe was filed to a thinner, sharper (and more delicate) edge for chopping clear wood (free of dirt and knots).

Parade Axes

The axe as an item of heraldry and celebration can be found around the world. Parade axes have been found on six continents, conveying messages of power, productivity, and patriotism. One such group that used parade axes more recently were the Modern Woodmen of America, a fraternal benefit society established in 1883 that had its members assemble into "forester drill teams" and perform in parades with their decorative cast aluminum axes.

BELOW: Decorative cast aluminum axes have become sought-after collectors' items. Note the MWA insignia near the poll of the axe.

LEFT: This fraternity sign would have been displayed in a meeting hall. The emblems of the Woodmen are the axe, with which European settlers cleared the forests; the wedge, which opened up the secret resources of nature; and the beetle or mallet, which represented progress.

BELOW: The axes only weighed about 1.5 pounds and were used for tricks, much like a baton. Note the forestry-themed insignias including the oak leaf cuffs and an axe/wedge/beetle belt buckle.

Axe Patterns

An axe "pattern" refers to the shape of an axe. Early American axes were developed on a local and regional scale and reflected the local preferences of lumberjacks. Not surprisingly, states with larger lumbering industries developed more axe patterns. In Maine for example, a dozen different Maine-specific patterns were developed, which reflected different regions and were probably used by axe makers as part of a selling scheme to boost sales.

The total number of axe patterns in existence isn't exactly clear for several reasons. First, some axe patterns are identical, despite having names that suggest different geographic points of origin (for example, the New England and Improved Wisconsin patterns are identical). Another challenge is that before axe production was industrialized in the 1850s, blacksmiths made custom axes that didn't neatly fit the established axe patterns that came later. Most axe collectors acknowledge about

60 unique single-bit American axe patterns and about 30 unique double-bit axe patterns. The key here is the word "unique," as some axe manufacturers claimed more than 300 patterns. Many of these were not truly different patterns, but simply different-sized heads of the same pattern, or axes being sold in different markets under different names.

The impressive variety of axe patterns has created a market for axe collectors who specialize in a single pattern, or conversely, aim to collect as many different patterns as possible. As you begin scrounging yard sales and antique stores, you'll soon discover that certain makers and patterns are more common than others. Patterns that were more intricate, having bevels or lugs for example, were more expensive and produced in smaller quantities. Simple patterns such as the Dayton and Michigan axe were produced in large numbers and are therefore more common.

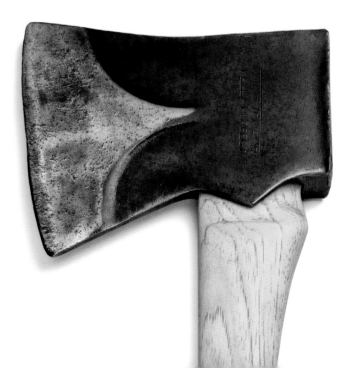

Axe patterns that are more distinct command higher prices from axe collectors. This large and near-mint Kelly Perfect Jersey bit was found in a hardware store that closed in the 1960s, where it sat undiscovered for decades.

Common American Axe Patterns

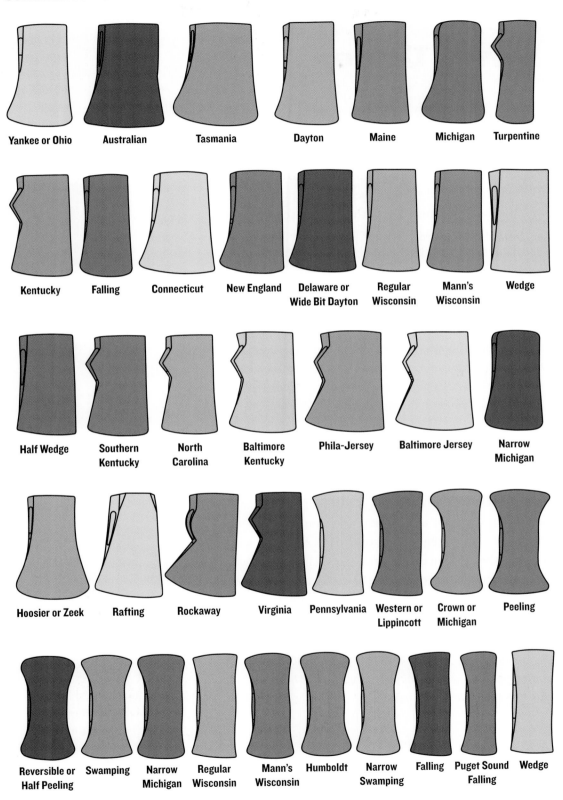

Yankee or Ohio	Australian	Tasmania	Dayton	Maine	Michigan	Turpentine

Kentucky	Falling	Connecticut	New England	Delaware or Wide Bit Dayton	Regular Wisconsin	Mann's Wisconsin	Wedge

Half Wedge	Southern Kentucky	North Carolina	Baltimore Kentucky	Phila-Jersey	Baltimore Jersey	Narrow Michigan

Hoosier or Zeek	Rafting	Rockaway	Virginia	Pennsylvania	Western or Lippincott	Crown or Michigan	Peeling

Reversible or Half Peeling	Swamping	Narrow Michigan	Regular Wisconsin	Mann's Wisconsin	Humboldt	Narrow Swamping	Falling	Puget Sound Falling	Wedge

Axes for Export Down Under

Although Paul Bunyan may be the quintessential American lumberjack, Australia and New Zealand arguably produce the world's finest axemen. The reason is both cultural and environmental. Wood chopping down under is akin to baseball in the United States; families spend weekends in the park picnicking at wood-chopping competitions that offer cash prizes and feature competitors sporting white Sunday pants — the true sign of a gentlemen's sport. The junior classes start children as young as eight in competition.

The second reason the Aussies and Kiwis are so good at wood chopping is that their competition wood — silver-top ash, among others — is incredibly hard and dense. You can't bull your way through the wood; it must be chopped with accuracy, precision, and technique. Compared to American axes, the Australian (and later New Zealand) axes were larger and heavier than their American counterparts, and specifically designed for chopping dense hardwood. Weighing in at 5-plus pounds, these Tasmanian-patterned axes had both the heft and bit width (6 inches or more) to efficiently chop wood.

The earliest recorded official wood-chopping championship dates to 1891 in Latrobe, Tasmania. This sporting spectacle is regarded by many as the event that spurred the development of the modern racing axe. Australian axe maker Hytest quickly became the name in competitive wood chopping, but American axe makers looking to increase brand recognition developed their own Tasmanian patterns, starting in the 1920s. Kelly Axe Works developed the Kelly Dandenong pattern, which was manufactured in Canada for the Australian market. Plumb also developed a number of early racing axes for both the domestic and international markets. Today they are sought after by both collectors and professional woodchoppers.

The Kelly Tasmanian quickly earned a reputation in the U.S. as a superior speed chopping axe. Although this pattern is similar to Connecticut pattern axes, it weighed nearly a pound more than most felling axes and quickly earned a spot at wood-chopping competitions around the world.

Standing block chop

Underhand chop

Lumberjacks at the 1956 Sydney World Championships compete in the three board jigger, the standing block chop, and the underhand chop. Competitors from "down under" customarily wear white trousers.

The Chainsaw Axe

Perhaps one of the most unique vintage axes ever made was the chainsaw or undercutter axe, which was first developed in the late 1930s by George Burns of Vancouver Island, British Columbia. This axe helped to bridge the transition in logging technology from axes and crosscut saws to the modern chainsaw.

The chainsaw axe was intended to be a complementary tool used in conjunction with early chainsaws, which weren't capable of making angled cuts when felling a tree. Up to this point the undercut — the first cut in the carefully angled notch that controls how the tree falls — was made with a chainsaw, but the angled notch itself still had to be chopped with an axe. The labor solution to this was to cut a series of parallel, horizontal cuts on the front of the tree and then use the prybar-like poll chisel to break out the wood, creating a block notch. If the notch needed to be cleaned up, the sharp bit was there to take care of the dirty work. The notch gave both direction and gravitational persuasion to the falling tree.

Within a decade, chainsaws had developed to the point that the chainsaw axe was obsolete, thanks to lighter, more maneuverable chainsaws and better chain technology that allowed for cutting the notch diagonally. These axes are now highly sought-after by collectors because of their rarity and interesting history.

Up until the advent of the modern chainsaw, the chainsaw axe was used to pry out the wedge during felling.

1965: The End of the Golden Axe Era

FOR MORE THAN TWO CENTURIES, the axe occupied a central role in settling, and literally building, America. However, by the early 1960s, it became clear that the axe was moving from a starring role to a minor character in the American landscape. The transition to chainsaws, migration from rural to suburban environments, and decline of wood heat all contributed to the end of the golden era of axes.

In an effort to stay afloat, axe manufacturers responded by merging companies, relocating to Asia and South America, and diversifying by making other tools. For those manufacturers who survived, it became clear that the American consumer was no longer a lumberjack who depended on a quality tool for his livelihood, and was instead more likely a suburbanite who was apt to use the axe for grubbing out an ornamental shrub in the lawn, or splitting a few pieces of wood on a summer camping trip. This led to a race to the bottom, resulting in cheap, inferior axes. And while consumers would like to blame the axe makers, we must acknowledge that our decreased demand for a quality American axe was the ultimate driver.

However, like the men who swung them even after the advent of the chainsaw, a few axe makers went against the grain and continued to make quality axes well into the power-saw era. Perhaps most famous was the Spiller Axe Company of Oakland, Maine, which continued to forge axes by hand until 1965.

This rare Spiller felling axe still has portions of the original paper label intact.

CHAPTER 3

AXES
FROM THE
GOLDEN
AGE OF
AXE-MAKING

O VER THE COURSE OF MY RESEARCH
I've asked fellow axe enthusiasts
to name the vintage axes they feel
are the most collectible. What makes an
axe collectible is somewhat subjective, but
I've done my best to consider the following
factors: rarity, demand, uniqueness, and
historical significance. All of the axes in this
chapter hail from the high-production era
of American axes, which spanned a century,
from the Civil War to the mid-1960s. Adding
to the excitement of collecting is the fact
that most of these axes can still be found
in unassuming places; all of the ones shown
in this chapter were found at garage sales,
estate auctions, and in the dirt below dilapi-
dated barns.

The Black Raven

The first time I saw a Kelly Black Raven axe was as a teenager. The old lumberjack who showed me the axe told me that he had bought it used at a barn sale for a dollar. He thought a dollar was rather high, but given that it had a new handle, he sprang for the axe. When I commented that I thought the "embossing" was beautiful, he corrected me and let me know that technically it was "etched," not "embossed." Apparently, the paper labels that were over the side of the eye used "embossed" or raised seals as a sign of quality and authenticity. That said, many collectors still use the term "embossed," which may be a useful search term (if not correct) for locating a Black Raven of your own.

The Black Raven axe was introduced by the Kelly Axe Manufacturing Company in 1904. The axe was manufactured at their foundry in Charleston, West Virginia, and was considered to be a premium axe, with some of the etchings gilded in gold paint (actually a mix of bronzing powder and varnish). These axes also seemed to receive more real estate in wholesale tool catalogues, often to the exclusion of other Kelly brands.

The Black Raven etching was found on single-bit felling axes, double-bit axes, hatchets, and, beginning in 1920, on scythes. The earlier Black Raven axes read "Kelly Axe Mfg. Co." directly under the raven. The later Black Raven axes read "The American Fork and Hoe Co" which was a separate branch of the company that took over in 1930. Additionally, these later Black Raven axes also included a "True Temper Kelly Works" etching near the poll of the single-bit axe, and on the opposite side as the raven etching on the double-bit axes. The smaller axes and hatchets used a circular etching of the raven.

It comes as little surprise that collectors would seek out the black raven since it is so distinct. As with all vintage axes, the price is heavily influenced by the condition of the axe. Pristine examples can bring auction prices north of $1,000. The good news is that collectors still report finding Black Raven axes at barn sales, auctions, and flea markets for a few dollars.

Arguably the most collectible of American axes, the Black Raven is sought after for its intricate etching that, to many people, represents a bygone era in American toolmaking.

The Plumb Champion

JUST AS CAR COMPANIES SPONSOR RACE CARS to highlight the superiority of their product, so too did the axe industry. Beginning in 1929, the Fayette R. Plumb Company of Philadelphia introduced the Champion Axe. It was considered a premium axe and was intended to promote an image of superiority in an axe market that, by the late 1920s, was beginning to get crowded. The introduction of the Plumb Champion also coincided with the emergence of competitive wood chopping as a sport — a high-visibility venue for promoting Plumb axes.

At that time (and still to this day), the most competitive woodchoppers came from Australia. Plumb sought out Peter McLaren, an Australian champion who had toured much of Europe as a circus and vaudeville axe performer. Plumb commissioned McLaren to be its spokesperson and developed the Champion Axe, which features an impressive etching of McLaren underhand chopping.

The promotional scheme was simple but effective. Hardware stores that sold Plumb axes would invite McLaren to come and compete against local talent. McLaren would use his

Peter McLaren, far left, teaches members of the Civilian Conservation Corps how to swing an axe.

Plumb axe and promised to chop the log in two-thirds of the time it took the other chopper to cut the log. The only rule was that the competitor couldn't use a Plumb axe against McLaren. The prize for beating McLaren started at $25 and was later increased to $50. There is no evidence that McLaren was ever beaten at one of these events, though choppers that came close were sometimes given a Plumb Champion axe as a runner-up prize.

The Plumb Champion axe promotion boosted sales of axes and helped to spread the sport of chopping worldwide. Plumb produced a series of larger racing axes for the Australian market, though none of them included the Champion etching.

The sales materials for the Plumb Champion advertised the axe at being designed for "expert choppers," though it appears Plumb was more than happy to sell it to anyone who had the money. The axe was available in both single- and double-bit designs and enjoyed a production run of more than 20 years, ending in 1951.

While the Champion axe would have originally been black with the etching lightly buffed, many of the Champion axes that turn up today have shallow etchings that have been further eroded by time. In my experience, finding a double-bit Champion in pristine condition is more difficult than finding a single-bit in equal condition because the high point of the eye is the same point as the chopper etching. The result is that as these axes were sharpened in a vise, the etching was often worn/damaged by the vice jaws. A pristine Champion axe will command nearly as much as a Kelly Black Raven.

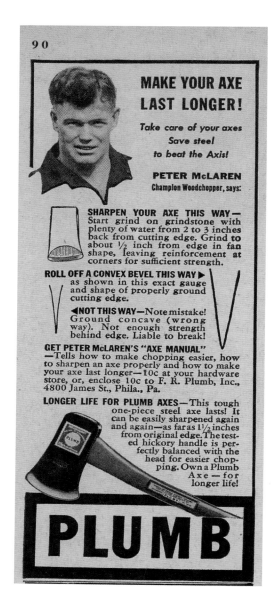

Peter McLaren became not just a brand ambassador for Plumb axes, but a role model and idol to the many Boy Scouts, Civilian Conservation Corps members, and loggers who attended his trainings and read his axe manual.

AXE MANUAL

OF PETER McLAREN

America's Champion Chopper

The Collins Legitimus

ONE OF THE CHALLENGES of producing a quality product is the risk of counterfeit goods being produced under your name. Such was the case for Collins & Company of Collinsville, Connecticut. Collins began producing quality axes in 1826 and went on to become one of the world's largest producers of edged tools. Beginning around 1845, axes started appearing in the marketplace bearing the Collins name, but were simply low-quality imposters. Three of the imposter companies were within a 150-mile radius of the Collins factory. At first public shaming through advertisements was employed, but the effects proved short-lived.

In 1875 Collins had had enough and developed a new trademark aimed squarely at counterfeiters. The etching (and embossing that appeared on paper labels) showed a flexed forearm raising a hammer above a crown. Below the crown was the word "Legitimus." To the surprise of many, the Legitimus marking proved successful in helping to curb counterfeits. In fact, the Legitimus label was used for 91 years, ending in 1966 when Collins was purchased by the Mann Edge Tool Company of Pennsylvania.

Because the Legitimus line ran for nearly a century, collectors have a good chance of finding a Collins Legitimus axe for a fair price. In addition to their interesting history, these axes are quality tools that can and should continue to be used. The axes were made with "crucible steel" which was essentially iron and other metals melted in batches and then forged into its final form as an axe. Like most foundries, Collins had their own crucible formula which created tools hard enough to hold a fine edge, yet soft enough to resist cracking.

The Collins Legitimus sported a small etching of a flexed forearm raising a hammer above a crown. The size, location, and intricacy of this logo was modified over time.

The Kelly Registered Axe

COMPETITION IN THE WORLD OF AXE-MAKING was at its height during the early twentieth century. Axe makers struggled to differentiate their products in a marketplace that was flooded with both legitimate competition from other axe makers, and a torrent of counterfeits. To reinforce the authenticity of their brand and to suggest a blacksmith's personal touch, the Kelly Registered Axe was developed. The early Registered axes listed the year they were made, with the serial number below. A number of circa 1915 Registered axes have appeared with "USA" listed alongside the year. The serial numbers were hand stamped and show considerable variation in the numbering style.

Later Registered axes did not include the year, and there are no known records that link the serial numbers to specific dates. However, in 1930 the Kelly Axe & Tool Co. was purchased by the American Fork & Hoe Company. Axe production was continued under the new name of the Kelly Axe & Tool Works. The American Fork & Hoe Co. eventually changed the name of the axe-making division, as well as some of their other divisions, to True Temper Corporation. The later Kelly Registered axes carried the True Temper/Kelly Works name above the Registered axe etching.

These axes almost always follow a Connecticut pattern. Their relatively large bit (some over 5 inches) meant that these axes were desirable in wood-chopping competitions prior to the development of specialized racing axes. Today, the Kelly Registered axe continues to grow in popularity.

Kelly Registered Axes were ostensibly numbered individually for purchasers. Even still, the number of axes they produced remains a mystery, as company records were either lost, or not thoroughly kept, as some axe historians have suggested.

The Winchester Axe

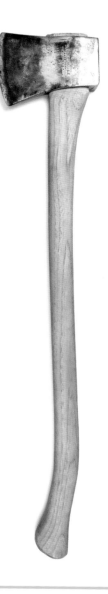

The Winchester Repeating Arms Company of New Haven, Connecticut, was founded in 1866 and quickly became an icon; the model '73 was a quick-firing lever-action rifle that earned the title of "the gun that won the West" due to its prevalence on the frontier.

During World War I, Winchester borrowed heavily to fund its expansion as a leading supplier of arms and ammunition to the federal government; as a result, Winchester had excessive production capacity when the war ended and tried to become a general manufacturer of consumer goods. It started The Winchester Store, through which consumers could buy virtually anything under the Winchester name. The original partnership included the axe maker E. C. Simmons & Company, but it was the equipment and facility from the former Mack Axe Company in Beaver Falls, Pennsylvania, that would become home to the Winchester axe in 1920.

Most of the Winchester axes produced were between 3 and 6 pounds, in addition to several smaller hatchets. As well as purchasing the Mack Axe Company, Winchester also purchased the Barney and Berry Company, which made quality hatchets carrying the Winchester logo. Over the eleven-year run, at least five different etchings appeared on Winchester axe heads. The handles of many of the Winchester axes bore a yellow label that read: "Head is forged from special steel. Handle is second growth hickory, split with the grain and secured with an interlocking wedge. This is an example of WINCHESTER quality."

The last of the Winchester axes and hatchets were produced in 1931. While not as rare as some axes, prices associated with the Winchester axe continue to climb, likely due to both axe and firearms collectors chasing the same limited supply. Of the Winchester axes, the large, 6-pound felling axe is the most uncommon.

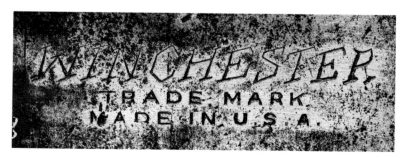

The Winchester name is best known for firearms, but expanding into other outdoor sporting goods and tools seemed like a logical extension in the 1920s. Winchester axe production lasted just over a decade, ending in 1931.

The Abercrombie Axe

TODAY, MOST PEOPLE ASSOCIATE THE ABERCROMBIE & FITCH NAME with high-end clothing that targets brand-conscious teenagers. However, the Abercrombie Company dates to 1892 (later named Abercrombie & Fitch in 1904), and had an outstanding reputation as a quality outfitter for expeditions and outdoor pursuits. David Abercrombie was a miner, trapper, and engineer who knew the value of quality equipment. When Abercrombie & Fitch couldn't manufacture equipment that their customers requested, they would partner with other companies and oversee production under the Abercrombie & Fitch name. Such was the case with axes. The primary axe-making partner for Abercrombie & Fitch was the Collins tool company of Collinsville, Connecticut (described on page 94). All of the axes made by Collins for Abercrombie & Fitch carried the famous Collins Legitimus logo on one side with the Abercrombie & Fitch logo on the other side of the poll.

Most of the Abercrombie & Fitch axes produced were camping axes or hatchets. The axes were sold with attractive leather scabbards that included a belt loop and decorative gold-and-black snap sporting the A&F logo.

In 30 years of axe collecting, I've only run across three Abercrombie & Fitch axes for sale. The axe pictured is one I purchased at auction. It had been found in the corner of an old Adirondack hardware store that featured a camping section. The axe head was still wrapped in its original paraffin paper under the leather sheath. Such a find is certainly rare, but also stands as a testament to the axe gems still waiting to be found.

Abercrombie & Fitch partnered with Collins to make a quality camping axe with the A&F logo on one side and the Collins Legitimus logo on the reverse side.

The Spiller Axe

OVER THE COURSE OF RESEARCHING this book I spoke with dozens of old lumberjacks and woodsmen and always asked their opinion for the best axe ever made. As you might imagine, there was no shortage of opinions. However, for those who had truly lived by their axe (pulp loggers and trappers throughout the Northeast), the name Spiller was repeatedly mentioned as one of the plainest (no fancy etchings) but finest axes made. It was the tempering of the steel that folks always mentioned — soft enough to file but hard enough to hold an edge, even in frozen wood.

Blacksmith Samuel Spiller got his start in the axe-making trade around 1813. Throughout his career, he made his way around lumber towns of the Northeast setting up shops in New Hampshire, Maine, and New Brunswick, Canada. His sons followed him into the blacksmithing trade, as did his grandson, Mark D. Spiller, who moved the company to Oakland, Maine.

While the axes themselves remained utilitarian, they were given names and paper labels that were meant to sell axes. These included the Choppers' Choice, The Maine Easy Cut, The Victory Axe, and The Pine Tree Clean Cut Axe.

Spiller continued to produce handmade axes in Oakland until 1965 — a 153-year run by a single family of axe makers. In the end, decreasing demand for axes and more efficient manufacturing processes left Spiller and other axe makers of central Maine unable to compete.

Spiller enjoyed an impressive 153-year run producing quality axes.

The Keen Kutter

For many axe collectors, their entry into this addictive obsession began with a Keen Kutter. The Keen Kutter first appeared as a brand of the Simmons Hardware Company in 1866. This St. Louis–based hardware giant reserved the Keen Kutter label for their highest-quality axes and cutlery.

In 1940 Simmons Hardware purchased rival toolmaker, Shapleigh Hardware, who retained the overall design of the Keen Kutter etching, but replaced the Simmons with Shapleigh. For axe collectors, these subtle changes serve as important reference points for dating axes. Shapleigh went out of business in 1960. The Keen Kutter trademark was purchased by Val-Test Distributors who dropped the Shapleigh name, but used the logo though the 1990s.

Keen Kutter axes came in virtually every imaginable size and pattern — from broadaxes to miniature hatchets, and from 6-pound single-bit Jersey axes to large double-bit axes with phantom bevels. Production numbers varied widely throughout the century-long production run of axes; the #4 felling axes and carpenter hatchets were manufactured in large numbers. Larger axes and those with more intricate designs (such as bevels and lugs) typically command higher prices.

Because Keen Kutter was a trademark applied to lots of products besides axes, it has developed cross-collectability. Some of the other items featuring the Keen Kutter trademark include: knives, drawshaves, wrenches, screwdrivers, razor blades, meat grinders, kitchen scales, hand planes, and padlocks. The popularity of vintage Keen Kutter tools has unfortunately created a market of counterfeits. The most commonly counterfeited Keen Kutter is a broadaxe that is made out of cast iron, instead of forged out of steel. Cast iron is noticeably more porous, and most of the reproductions also have crude casting marks from the mold. For more information on collecting Keen Kutter axes and tools, as well as the latest information on counterfeits, check out The Hardware Companies Kollectors Klub online.

Capitalizing on the success of their Keen Kutter axes, the Simmons Hardware Company expanded the Keen Kutter label to include a variety of tools, such as the hand plane, pliers, and pipe wrench shown above.

The Sager Chemical is one of the few axes where the production year is included below the maker's mark. This has encouraged axe-oholics to pursue "vertical collections," similar to collecting vintage wine.

The Sager Chemical Axe

THE STORY OF THE SAGER CHEMICAL PROCESS AXE began in 1893 when William Sager, along with his three sons, founded the Warren Axe & Tool Company in Warren, Pennsylvania. In 1895 Sager was granted a patent for a tool finish that promised to prevent rust and prolong the life of the axe. The two-part procedure consisted of dipping the heated block of steel into an (unknown to us) chemical mixture. The second part was a quenching process that resulted in the axe taking on a deep blue color, similar to the bluing found on firearms.

While Sager's chemical process appears to have been adopted by the Louisville Axe & Tool Company which he worked for later on, the Sager Chemical axe continued to be manufactured by Warren. From 1914 to 1950 many of the Sager Chemical axes were marked with the year of manufacture. In the axe world this was unique since the year an axe was made was seen as irrelevant to the user. However, for collectors this information is invaluable to understanding the history of these companies and the evolution of the axe.

In recent years the Sager Chemical axe has surged in popularity — particularly the large (#4) Puget Sound pattern axes that were made for felling large timber in the Pacific Northwest. Another popular pattern is the bow tie or peeler axe that features a wide (5½-inch) symmetrical bit. These axes are sought after by competitive and backyard lumberjacks looking for a well-balanced and affordable throwing axe.

Similar to wine, the concept of a developing a vertical Sager Chemical axe collection has appeared on a number of the online axe forums. To date, I am only aware of two complete Sager Chemical axe collections with every year from 1914 to 1950 represented. While the 1914–1920 axes are extremely rare, the later axes are fairly common. Both single-bit and double-bit axes were made (as well as a few specialized axes like the chainsaw axe), but the double-bit axes are certainly more prevalent than the single-bit axes.

The Sager Chemical Axe was available in a variety of single- and double-bit patterns, as well as the short-lived chainsaw axe pattern (bottom).

The Lincoln Axe

OF ALL THE ETCHED AXES, the Lincoln axe takes the cake for the most intricate (and most words — 25) in an etching. While the evolution of the Lincoln axe is complicated and involved a number of manufacturers, the image etched on the side of the Lincoln axe made it quite clear that customers were purchasing an axe as trustworthy and authentic as Honest Abe himself.

The Lincoln axes were manufactured under contract for hardware companies by the Mann Edge Tool Company of Lewistown, Pennsylvania. Mann first made the Lincoln axe for the Schreiber, Conchar & Westphal Company (S.C.W.) in 1893 and continued for a decade. In 1904, A. Tredway & Sons Hardware acquired the Schreiber, Conchar & Westphal Company. Under this acquisition the Lincoln axe etching was modified to reflect the new ownership, but it didn't show up as a new etching until 1907. The A. Tredway & Sons Hardware designation was carried on the Lincoln axe until 1929 when a new partnership, the Kretschmer-Tredway Hardware Company, carried the Lincoln axe line.

To many, the Lincoln axe is considered the holy grail of axe collecting. The early Schreiber, Conchar & Westphal Company Lincoln axe is the rarest, and commands a small fortune. All of the Lincoln axes were available in both single- and double-bit, though the double-bit axes seem to appear more frequently.

Few names could evoke the image of quality and honesty like Abraham Lincoln. The Schreiber, Conchar & Westphal Company (and later Tredway & Sons Hardware) took full advantage of this in marketing their axes.

Give me six hours to chop down a tree and I will spend the first four sharpening the axe.
— Abraham Lincoln

Our Very Best Axe

THE OUR VERY BEST or OVB axe was offered by the Chicago hardware giant Hibbard, Spencer, Bartlett and Company, which eventually became True Value Hardware. The first OVB axes were offered from the mid-1880s to the early 1960s. The early OVB axes had an intricate etching consisting of a large shield with a banner that read "OVB" with an overlay banner "Our Very Best" and a top banner "HSB & CO." Later OVB axes sported an equally large etching that was square and was intended to be more contemporary, with angled "OVB" letters and "Hibbard Spencer Bartlett & Co" spelled out.

Based on advertising literature, it appears that OVB single-bit axes were available in three patterns: Michigan, Dayton, and Wisconsin. By far, the most common single-bit pattern was the Michigan. The OVB was also available as a double-bit axe in the Michigan pattern.

One interesting bit of lore surrounding this axe deals with the claim made in the name. Apparently, early critics found "Our Very Best" to be a bit humble, and felt that it almost begged the question, "well, what is THE best?" By the 1890s advertising for OVB axes included a line that read: "The truth: our very best is the best axe." This axe-iom continued to be included on advertising materials for decades.

OVB axes are not as rare as many of the other axes included in this section but, with their intricate etching and fascinating history of humblebrag, are considered a must-have collector's axe.

The etching on this axe went through at least two different iterations in an attempt to present a modern appearance.

DCH Clean Cut Clover Axe

Founded in 1888, Dunham, Carrigan & Hayden (DCH) was the leading supplier of wholesale hardware in San Francisco at the turn of the century, until closing in 1927. As a West Coast purveyor of fine tools, the DCH's Clean Cut axe earned a reputation for quality. Among their most popular axes was a giant California reversible double-bit pattern. This axe measured more than 10 inches long, had 5-inch cutting bits, and weighed almost 5 pounds.

The etching of a four-leaf clover on the side of the axe led to it being referred to as the "lucky axe." Given the lore and superstition surrounding these axes, it was a pretty clever marketing strategy. At least three other brands used a lucky clover image in their labels and etchings, as well. Most of the DCH axes are dated on the side opposite the logo etching. The dates are presented in two digits (e.g., "05" = 1905.) In addition to large double-bit axes, the DCH Clean Cut Clover axe was also available in several single-bit felling patterns, as well as hatchets.

If an axe can be lucky, the Clean Cut Clover Axe must be the luckiest.

The Kelly Flint Edge

THE KELLY FLINT EDGE makes for an ideal first collector's axe, because of its prevalence and the number of patterns available. Its high-quality steel also makes it an excellent work axe. The Flint Edge brand persisted from the mid-1880s, through the late 1950s. During that time, the brand was trademarked property that was owned by several different manufacturers, who made minor modifications to the etchings and paper labels. The paper labels, and later the cheek etchings, featured an axe maker tempering the "flint edge" in a chemical bath. Later True Temper Flint Edge axes used a stencil to paint a flint arrow head on the cheek of the axe. These axes were widely promoted by print advertisements.

The early Flint Edge axes shared many characteristics with the Kelly Perfect axe, which featured beveled cheeks and virtually all of the same patterns across the two brands. The patterns that are most collectible for the Flint Edge axes include an oversized Connecticut pattern and Puget Sound pattern.

Axe Superstitions

There is no shortage of superstitious uses for the axe. In Mexico an axe is sometimes placed bit-up in a field to protect the harvest from bad weather. In aboriginal Australia, throwing axes as the sky darkens was seen as a way to scare away the storm gods. In more modern times the American lumberjack was warned about leaving his axe in a stump, as it was thought to bring bad luck and invite logging accidents.

Later Flint Edge axes included a stenciled arrowhead design that was painted, not etched.

The Norlund Trailblazer

In 1965 the Canadian Tire Co. approached the management of the Mann Edge Tool Company in Lewistown, Pennsylvania, with a proposal that Mann manufacture a line of "Sportsmen's Axes" to be sold alongside other outdoor equipment at Canadian Tire. As the story goes, John Waddell, the president of the Mann Edge Tool Company, had traveled to Sweden and admired the small but versatile Scandinavian-styled axes. By December 1968 the O. A. Norlund Company had been officially established and made not just axes and hatchets, but also fishing and camping equipment.

The company quickly gained a following in Canada and was then was more widely distributed through hardware stores in the United States. The most popular pattern produced by Norlund was 1.25-pound Voyager hatchet. Their light weight, quality steel, and leather sheath made them the choice of many campers. Less common, and as a result increasingly desirable, the two-pound Norlund Trailblazer became a favorite of trail crews and foresters as a lightweight work axe.

While the Norlund axes and hatchets are considerably newer than many of the other collectible axes, they have emerged as must-have axes because they were one of the last mass-produced quality American axes. Interestingly, prices for the Norlund Trailblazer appear to be rising as those participating in competitive lumberjack sports have identified the Trailblazer as an ideal throwing axe when matched with a 24-inch handle.

The Trailblazer is a versatile axe that can be used for both camp chores and camp games.

The President's Hunting Axe

IN AUGUST OF 1902, PRESIDENT THEODORE ROOSEVELT took a train trip through New England that included a stop in Waterville, Maine. Upon disembarking, Roosevelt was presented with a "hunting axe" as a souvenir from Maine's axe-making mecca. The axe, which is technically a hatchet, sported an oak and walnut handle that included a hunting knife with brass ferrule. As the President left Waterville, Maine, it was reported by *The Pittsburgh Press* that Roosevelt "waived his little axe triumphantly at the crowd as the train pulled out."

Less than three weeks after President Roosevelt received the axe, his Assistant Secretary, William Lobe, Jr. sent a letter at the President's request asking John King to make a "hatchet like that which the President has" for Kermit Roosevelt, Theodore's son.

Although the location of the President's original hunting axe isn't known, it is thought that there are at least five others that exist today. The axe was sold to the general public as the Sportsmen's Axe, though its informal moniker as the President's Hunting Axe held. Originally the axe sported a paper label with a moose, and was made under the King & Roy name, as well as the later King Axe Co. The earlier axes had "King & Roy" engraved on the knife. If you find this axe, you've hit the jackpot.

This hatchet, which featured a hidden hunting knife, became known as the President's Hunting Axe after axemaker John King presented it as a personal gift to Theodore Roosevelt in 1902.

CHAPTER 4

MODERN AXES

THE RECENT INTEREST IN TRADITIONAL TOOLS has inspired independent black-smiths, boutique axe makers who turn out a few dozen axes per year, and a few mass-producers of premium axes that are specifically designed for discerning woodsmen. Even large-scale American tool companies, such as Council Tool, have developed premium axes to bring quality axe-making back to America, albeit at a much smaller production level. While many of these axes are readily available on the market, it is likely that they will become future collectibles.

The Mountain Maul

Typically weighing between 6 to 16 hefty pounds, the maul relies on its mass and thick wedge to pop apart blocks of wood. Although I own a maul, it usually stays tucked in the barn, reserved for gnarly, knotted pieces that would swallow a smaller splitting axe.

Perhaps one of the most interesting modern splitting mauls is the Mountain Maul made by Warren Tool Company. This maul is unique in that it sports two bits at different angles. This gives the splitter two different options based on wood species and density. The handle of this maul was made nearly twice as wide as other maul handles, making it more forgiving in the event that the splitter suffered too long of a swing and struck the handle. The intricate etching, coupled with the fact that production of these mauls has ceased (originally patented in 1982 and only produced for a few years), has resulted in commanding prices for this unique maul of rather late origin.

A cousin to the maul is the splitting wedge, which is indispensable when it comes to splitting crotches and knotty whorls. Remember, the densest and most BTU-rich part of the log is where the knots are, so take the time to split these sections.

The option of a wide angle or narrow angle bit make this maul suitable for splitting both dense and softer wood species.

The Chopper One
Hybrid Splitting Axe

THE CHOPPER ONE SPLITTING AXE represents a hybrid between a maul, felling axe, and crowbar. The Chopper One was developed in 1975 by Bob Kolonia who noticed that when he struck a log at a slight angle, he was able to flick off pieces of firewood with ease. That inspired him to head to his workshop and ultimately develop the Chopper One patented axe. The axe uses rotating levers on each side of the axe's head. When the bit enters the wood, the levers swing out, directing the downward chopping force outward, splitting the log. While originally sold at big-box stores such as Sears and J. C. Penny, the axe was discontinued in the late 1980s. However, Bob has once again entered the axe-making world and now sells the Chopper One directly to consumers through his website.

The energy crisis of the early 1970s brought renewed dependence on wood heat that promoted the development of several hybrid splitting axes, including the Chopper One.

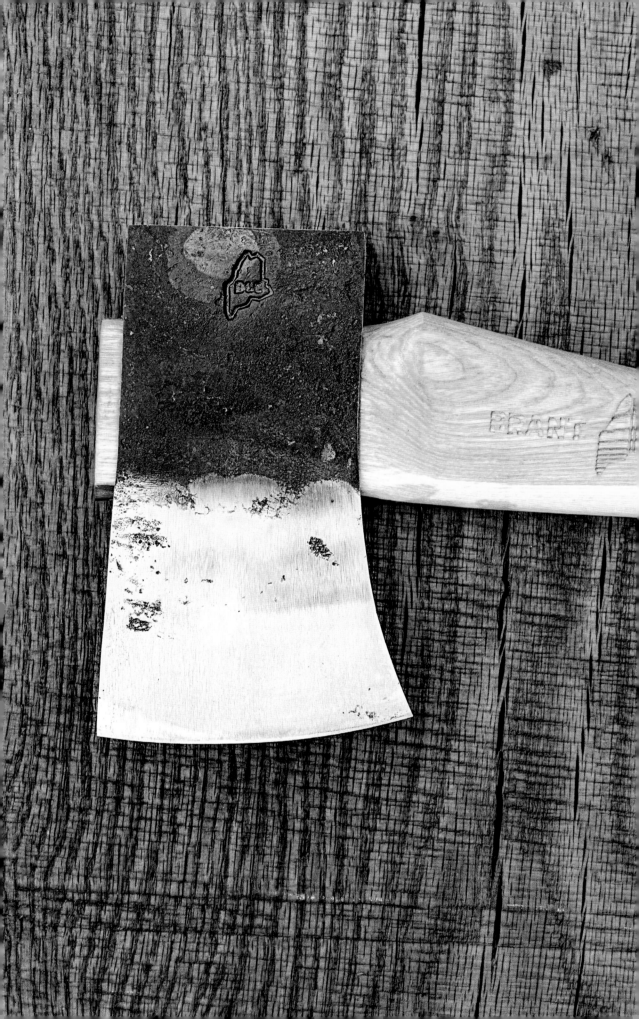

A Modern Camp Axe: The Allagash Cruiser

IN 2012, STEVE FERGUSON'S GODSON was graduating from high school and planning to go to forestry school at Paul Smith's College in the Adirondacks, so Steve thought buying a good American-made axe would be an appropriate graduation gift. Heading to his nearby hardware and outdoor stores in Maine, Steve was distressed to find few American-made options. He was inspired to start Brant & Cochran — now the only axe manufacturer in Maine, a state that once boasted almost 200 of them.

Brant & Cochran operates out of its South Portland, Maine, shop where it forges the Allagash Cruiser — the only Maine wedge-pattern camp axe being made today. Technically, this is a boy's axe, weighing in at 2½ pounds. It's made of high-quality 1050 carbon steel, and hangs on a beautiful 28-inch white ash handle that is made on Brant & Cochran's vintage handle duplicating lathe. The wedge pattern is simple, but effective; the poll is thicker than on most axes of this size, giving it extra heft. The result is deeper penetration with each blow of the axe.

Brant & Cochran manufactures and restores axes using time-tested techniques and the highest-quality American-made materials. Because it's such a labor-intensive process, they don't try to compete with foreign axe makers on price. Instead, they're making a quality Maine axe that can be handed down for generations.

The Brant & Cochran Allagash Cruiser is hand forged in Portland, Maine.

The Axe-Built Campfire

The edge of a razor sharp camp axe can be used to make curly tinder using a shaving motion. ▶

Small kindling or "pencils" are made by splitting in opposite directions and then peeling them apart. ▶

Firewood is laid "log-cabin" style, with a base of larger fuelwood and alternating layers of kindling. The interior is filled with shavings. ▶

A file brazed to the poll of this axe offers a coarse surface for lighting a "strike-anywhere" match. ▶

Within a couple of minutes, the campfire is ablaze. As the smaller kindling burns, it falls to the fire's center, adding additional fuel. ■

The Carving Axe

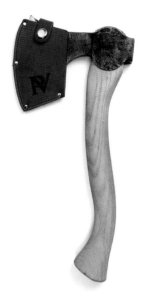

Once considered too crude and clunky for fine woodworking, the axe has earned a new reputation as the most essential tool of the greenwood craftsperson. Working with green or freshly cut wood requires a different set of tools than when working with dry wood. Axes excel at cutting diagonally through grain that's still wet, while the gullets of a saw would simply clog with wet wood.

The earliest of greenwood carving axes were the trade axes of the French and Portuguese. They featured small iron heads with hardened steel bits that could be honed to a razor edge. These trade axes would be used for any number of greenwood tasks, from carving clubs and tent stakes to spoons and stirrers. The modern carving axe has evolved to include a number of specialized improvements that are meant to make carving more efficient and precise. These improvements include: a double-bend handle that provides a comfortable grip closer to the axe head for more precise work, and lower grip position for splitting; a broad bearded bit that allows for shaving a flat surface; and a thin polished bit. Most of these modern carving axes are hand forged, with the waiting list for some axes extending a year or more.

Paul Krzyszkowski is one of North America's foremost makers of carving axes. His blacksmithing business started with his passion for woodcarving and his desire to make his own carving tools. Today, he has a thriving business called Toronto Blacksmith, and he makes small-batch, hand-forged carving axes. His axes are often based on odd vintage axe patterns; he loves the process of remaking them, understanding the original use, and the original tools used to create them.

One of his recent favorite axes is the Russian Topor, which has a distinct "tail" in front of the eye. This style of axe is distinct to Russia and lends itself well to limbing, carpentry, and carving work. Some of his most popular items are his curved, Viking-inspired axes — an aesthetically pleasing divergence from the simple wedge shape so common in most modern axes.

A carving axe makes quick work of roughing out a spoon that will be finished with a sloyd carving knife.

The Racing Axe

COMPETITIVE WOOD CHOPPING in the United States started with clever logging-camp foremen in the late 1800s, who would encourage competitiveness as a way to both feed the egos of their men, and boost production. Most early chopping races were informal events that used the same work axes for racing.

In the 1940s and 1950s, a number of competitive collegiate wood-chopping teams emerged, which helped to formalize wood chopping as a competitive sport. Colleges such as Dartmouth, West Point, and Paul Smith's emerged as powerhouses in the sport and fueled the professional ranks with capable axe men and women. With more than 60 colleges competing nationwide, this spurred demand for quality axes — at a time when the American axe market was declining and manufacturers were more focused on cutting costs and diversifying their product lines with other tools.

The formation of the Stihl Timbersports Series in 1986 brought competitors from around the world to the U.S. for lucrative lumberjack competitions. Australian axe maker Keesteel and New Zealand axe maker Tuatahi were able to capture 99 percent of this elite wood-chopping market with their quality racing axes. American woodchoppers felt that this gave competitors from down under an advantage in terms of both axe supply and trade knowledge.

Requests by American competitors looking to compete with American-made axes were met with the same response from American toolmakers: there just isn't enough demand to justify the high production costs. Then, in the early 2000s, a young professional competitor from New York State developed a Computer Numeric Control (CNC) technique that could cut an axe head out of a block of alloy, instead of having to cast or forge the head. The axe blanks could then be heat-tempered, ground, and polished to a mirror shine. The result was the American-made Brown Racing Axe.

Since then, others have adopted similar techniques which have allowed for the development of a small but robust American racing axe market. The Vermont Mold & Tool Company released the Vermont Racing Axe in 2018, which has given American woodchoppers yet another quality racing axe option. California-based Precision Axes worked directly with Stihl Timbersports competitor Walt Page to develop a formidable racing axe.

Racing axes use harder alloys than work axes do, have tighter manufacturing tolerances, and are ground to cut specific species of wood.

A racing axe in the hands of an accomplished chopper can cut several inches of wood with a single blow.

Mod Axes

For those looking for a truly one-of-a-kind axe, consider the custom or mod (modified) axe. These highly personalized axes may have a modified head, handle, or both. Many are made from old axe heads that are worn beyond repair. A good mod axe maker is able to see the possibilities, and work around the damage to identify a new pattern within the old axe. Depending on how much metal needs to be removed, the tool of choice may be an angle grinder, hacksaw, or cutting torch.

If you choose to modify your own axe, I suggest learning as much as you can about the axe before taking the grinder to it. I once discovered a Black Raven axe that someone decided to modify by grinding away the etching (and much of the axe's value). Here are some of the most common axe modifications.

Handles. Moving beyond the hardware store options, there are a variety of choices, including laminated handles, epoxy handles, pistol-grip handles, exotic hardwoods, and repurposed handles such as baseball bats. Studs, wenge (tapered)

plugs, and lanyards are also popular additions.

Wedges. One sign of the quality of axe work is the eye wedge. The wedge serves the important role of keeping the handle tight to the head. A variety of hardwoods with contrasting colors can be used to offset your hanging job. There are also steel, aluminum, and bronze wedges that can add a decorative touch.

Finishes. Depending on whether you want a mirror polish on your axe, weathered patina, or scalloped grooves, you'll need to use different tools and techniques.

Scary-sharp edges. Most new axes don't arrive razor sharp, and with good reason. To achieve a scary-sharp edge, the bit must be razor thin. This means that knots, frozen wood, or dirt can seriously damage the axe, and require repairs that reduce the overall longevity by shortening the bit, so something less than "scary sharp" may be ideal for a work axe. However, for specific tasks, and to impress your friends, consider trying the various methods of sharpening beginning on page 163.

ABOVE: An African padauk wedge adds a nice contrast to the white ash haft.

RIGHT: This Rooster Mod Chicken-Hawk hatchet started life as a Wards Master Quality half-hatchet.

LEFT: A rough-turned handle accented with a torch

LEFT: Identification stripes, to make it easier to find your axe in the woods

RIGHT: Counter-sink marks, to provide additional grip

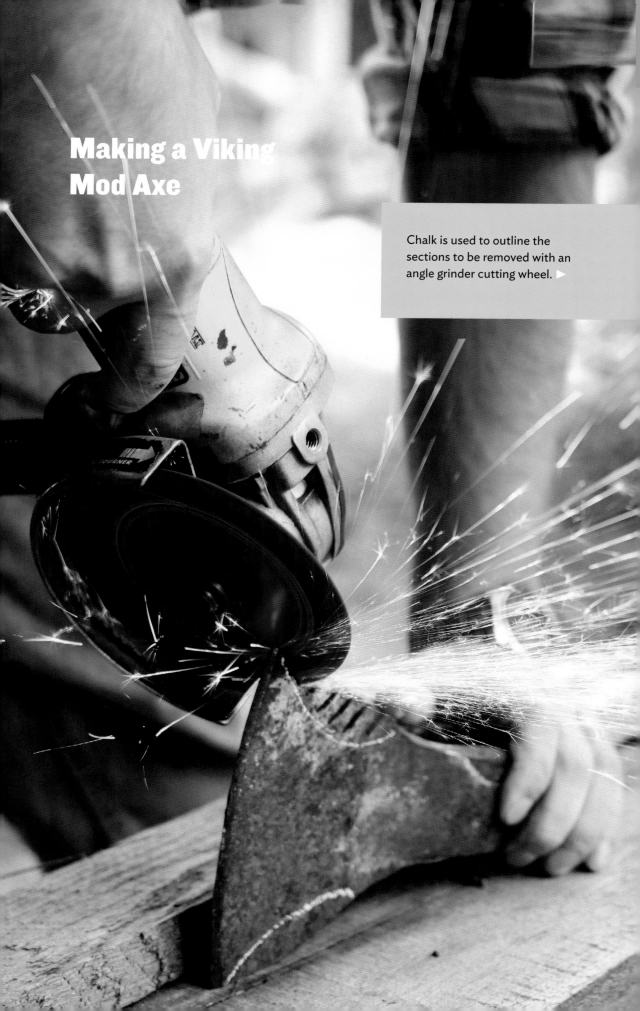

Making a Viking Mod Axe

Chalk is used to outline the sections to be removed with an angle grinder cutting wheel. ▶

The final contour is set using a flap wheel. It's important to proceed slowly at this stage; heating up the axe too much can ruin the temper. ▶

A propane torch can be used to add char for character. The torch should be moved quickly, and a wet rag should be kept handy (for obvious reasons). ▶

Light sanding is followed by a coat of linseed oil to finish the handle of this Mod Axe. ■

The Rooster Mod Axe-Aroon

CRAIG ROOST (A.K.A. "ROOSTER") is one of the administrators for the Axe Junkies online, and you might say axes are in his blood. He grew up in rural Wisconsin with an axe in his hands from the age of eight. By age twenty, Roost was working as a carpenter and quickly established himself as a proficient hewer, reconstructing many antique barns, as well as a log cabin dating to 1842. Along the way, Rooster developed a habit of picking up old axes at flea markets and restoring them for resale. Eventually this hobby grew to include modifying axes, appropriately known as Rooster Mod Axes.

A Rooster Mod Axe is a custom work of art. In some cases, his customers are looking to have an old family heirloom restored; in other cases, it's more about function, as was the case in making the Rooster Mod Axe-Aroon, which is a cross between a splitting axe and a pickaroon — the ultimate firewood tool.

Rooster's axe addiction eventually led him to a career with The Council Tool Co., where he works as supply chain manager and axe designer. Rooster was influential in the development of the new Flying Fox Woodsmen Hatchet as well as the redesign of the iconic Velvicut axe, which show a clear Rooster Mod influence.

RIGHT: This axe-aroon prototype made by Council Tool Co. Axe Designer Craig Roost, was made from a boy's axe head and a pick from a multi-tool. It's hung on a cut-down single-bit handle.

The Council Tool Co. Velvicut Premium line includes the Double Bit Saddle Axe, which weighs in at two pounds and sports phantom bevels for deep penetration and easy release from the wood.

The Council Tool Co. Flying Fox Woodsmen Hatchet is the SUV of the axe world. It features a rare beefy hardened poll that can be used as a hammer. It's also well suited as a bushcraft hatchet and is perfectly balanced for competitive hatchet throwing.

CHAPTER 5

RESTORING VINTAGE AXES

ANYONE CAN WHIP OUT THEIR CREDIT CARD AND BUY A NEW AXE, but certified Axe Junkies face uncontrollable excitement when they spot a dark corner at the flea market filled with rusty, broken-handled axes. This, my friends, is the intersection of opportunity and euphoria. Once you've made the deal, or have struck rusty gold digging at an old barn site, it's time to start the restoration. Since the axe you start with is likely to be coated with a thick coat of rust, treat this as if you're an archeologist, peeling back the layers of oxidation without damaging the steel (including any etchings) below. In a matter of hours, most axes can be transformed back into a work axe that's ready for another century of use — or simply a mantel piece to be admired.

Finding Vintage Axes to Restore

Seeking out old axes and restoring them is well worth your time. It's estimated that from 1850 to 1950 more than 10 million felling axes were produced by hundreds of different axe manufacturers. During this period, manufacturers had easy access to quality steel, and competition among forges meant that the quality of axes produced remains unprecedented to this day. Relatively few high-quality felling axes are still made, but barns and basements continue to be great places to find a quality vintage axe just begging for a second chance.

Six-Point Axe Inspection

Finding a vintage axe to restore is easy if you know what to look for. Don't get hung up on the state of the handle. In most cases, the old handle will be brittle, cracked, or rotted near the eye, and you'll need to replace it. Instead, the focus should be on finding a salvageable axe head.

Size. A standard felling axe weighs 3½ pounds. A longer, thinner-bitted axe will slice through wood more easily, while a short, chunky axe is better suited for splitting, where you're not actually cutting the wood but simply "popping" the wood apart along the grain.

Numbers etched on the cheek of the axe often reference the approximate weight of the axe. The larger number is pounds and the smaller number is understood to be the denominator under one, so this would be a three and one-half pound axe.

Markings. Virtually all quality axe manufacturers included their name or etching on the cheek of the axe; in some cases, a bit of steel wool is needed to reveal a clear enough stamp/etching to identify the maker. Some of the more notable makers, who used high-quality steel in their axes, were Plumb, Kelly-True Temper, Mann, Collins, and Council.

Bit condition. The bit of the axe is where the work is done, so it's important that the bit is relatively free of chips. A chipped bit will create resistance, known as drag, when you try to chop. Therefore, it becomes necessary to grind the bit until the chip is gone. The problem is that grinding the axe creates a shorter, stouter bit that doesn't cut very well.

Toe arc. The toe should carry the same arc as the rest of the bit. If it's rounded off, that's a telltale sign that the axe has been used for cutting roots or maybe even sharpening rocks. This is problematic because an overly rounded bit coming in contact with a round log increases the odds of the axe "glancing," or deflecting in an unsafe direction as the two rounded surfaces make contact.

Markings

Chipped bit

Worn toe

Warped eye

"Mushroomed" poll

Eye condition. The eye is the only point of contact between the handle and the head of the axe. An eye that is even slightly out of plumb means that the axe will never swing true, creating just enough deviation in the swing to cause the axe to glance, and potentially score a date with your shin. There are two potential causes for an untrue eye. The first is a defect in the manufacturing process. When an axe is made, the eye is generally cut using a punch. If the punch is not perfectly aligned, an off-center eye will result. The second is a result of misusing the axe as a sledge-hammer. Because the steel on the sides of the eye needs to be thin to achieve a narrow profile, it is particularly susceptible to bending and warping. This deformation often prevents the handle from fitting properly. It's best to avoid any axe that shows an off-center or deformed eye.

Poll condition. The poll is located directly behind the eye of the axe and is commonly "mushroomed" as a result of the axe being used as a sledgehammer. In cases of minimal damage, the burred edges can be lightly ground. In other cases, hair-line cracks may extend from the eye into the poll or the eye may be deformed, as described in the preceding paragraph. As a general rule, axes with severe mushrooming and cracks should be avoided.

A New Handle for An Old Axe

IF AN OLD HAFT, OR HANDLE, shows any signs of deterioration (cracks, a loose head, or a rotted eye), you should begin your restoration by fitting a new handle that you can safely clamp in a vise when you need to sharpen the head of the axe later on. "Hanging an axe," as woodsmen often call the process of fitting a handle, is as much of a skill as swinging or sharpening an axe; it requires both patience and practice.

The expression "to get the hang of it" originated with lumberjacks who were referring to a proper union between haft and head. If a haft fit poorly, the jack would often proclaim, "I just can't get the hang of it," meaning "I just can't get it right."

Removing the Old Handle

A common temptation is to toss the head in the fire to burn out the old handle, but this is a bad idea. Doing so changes the temper of the axe, in most cases making it more brittle and prone to cracking. Instead, the old haft should be sawed off and removed from the top down.

Pry or drill out the wedges. If the wooden wedges in the top of the handle are dry and brittle, they can be pried out with a screwdriver or chisel. If the wedges are firmly in place, it's best to use a drill to remove enough wood so that the plug can be popped out. Drill from both the top and the bottom of the head.

Driving out the
handle

Drive out the handle. After the wedges are removed, the head is then placed on two wood blocks, so that the handle can be driven out with a hammer and a "drift" — a block of wood or steel that is slightly smaller than the eye of the axe. For axes that have a larger eye at the top of the head than the bottom, the head needs to be flipped over to drive out the handle.

Selecting a New Handle

To finish your axe restoration, select a new, high-quality, hardwood handle that is straight and has the right grain orientation.

Straightness. Handles are generally sawn out of hickory or ash logs and then turned on a duplicating lathe. Depending on where the tree grew and how the log was sawn, the handle may twist or bow. With the exception of broadaxes, which have intentionally curved handles, replacement handles should be examined for trueness. By holding the eye of the handle just below your eye, visualize an imaginary line from end to end. Does the handle hold true to that line, or does it bow either left or right, or twist? Only straight and true axe handles should be used; a twisted or curved handle can make the axe glance, causing injury.

Grain orientation. The end of the axe handle is known as the "doe's foot" and will indicate which way the grain runs. Ideally, the grain should run parallel to the bit of the axe. Handles in which the grain runs perpendicular to the bit are inherently weak and snap under percussion.

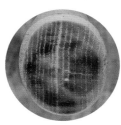

Proper grain orientation

Improper grain orientation

Growth-ring width and quality.
Tight, narrow rings indicate slower-growing wood, which makes for a stronger handle. The color of the wood is also important: Is one side of the handle dark wood and the other side light wood? The dark wood represents heartwood, which is dense but brittle. The lighter wood is the more recently grown sapwood, which is strong and flexible. An axe handle made entirely of sapwood is best; one made of both sapwood and heartwood is more likely to fracture.

Hanging the Handle

Although much attention is given to sharpening axes, hanging the axe properly is just as essential. If a head is hung crooked, the axe will glance off the wood. If it's hung too high or too low, it's susceptible to breaking. And if a handle with defects is used, you'll likely find yourself repeating the hanging process sooner than you'd like.

Fit the eye. File the eye of the handle with a rasp until the axe head fits on the shoulder of the handle; the fit may have to be fine-tuned to get the handle to hang perfectly straight. Check for trueness by aligning your eye with the axe head and looking down the handle.

Mark and cut. Mark the head location on the handle. The wedge slit can be extended with a thin-bladed handsaw, if necessary; it should extend to within ½ inch of the bottom of the axe head. Any excess handle above the axe head should be cut off.

Fitting the eye

Marking the head location

What to Do with Crooked Handles?

The handles of used axes that have spent years stowed in a damp corner may develop several inches of sweep or curvature. While this may not be suitable for a felling axe, these curved handles make great offset handles for hewing axes. Crooked handles at the hardware store can be a bargain, too. Store managers are usually very happy to have them out of inventory and will usually let them go for a 50 to 75 percent discount.

Drive the head. With the axe handle fitted into the head, pound the doe's foot with a rubber or wooden mallet. This drives the head onto the handle.

Drive the wedge. When the handle of the axe hangs true (straight or plumb), drive in the wooden wedge with a mallet. Saw off the top of the seated wedge with a coping saw.

A coat of oil. A coat of linseed oil will help keep an untreated handle from becoming brittle or cracked. If the new handle is finished, medium-grit sandpaper can be used to remove the varnish, so that the wood can be treated with linseed oil. (Varnish can make for a dangerously slick axe handle in wet conditions.)

Driving the head

Driving the wedge

Restoring the Axe Head

Beginning an axe restoration with a new handle means that there is now a dependable point from which to clamp, hold, and work on the axe. To preserve the new handle, clamp it in a bench vise using a shop rag. The middle third of the handle is the best clamping location, because it's the straightest part.

Remove the Rust

You'll want to begin by removing the surface rust, which can be done by hand with a sanding block but is much more effective using either a belt sander or an orbital sander. If your axe looks more like a relic from a shipwreck than a trusty tool, consider starting with 80-grit sandpaper. Start

lightly, keeping an eye out for manufacturing marks. If you find any, lightly hand-sand these areas using steel wool.

After removing the surface rust, you'll have a better idea what you're dealing with. Deeply pitted axes may prove unserviceable, though in most cases these axes may be resurrected by using a more aggressive grit of sandpaper and additional elbow grease. Cleaning up the cheeks of the axe is important, because this is the part of the axe that is in greatest contact with the kerf (or cut surface) of the log. Any pitting or remaining rust will serve as an abrasive, making the axe stick.

Once you've removed the majority of the rust with 80-grit sandpaper, move

to 120-grit sandpaper. As you continue to clean the axe, maintain light pressure and make sure you don't allow the sander to catch the bit. Also, if you're using an orbital sander, make sure it's continually moving; you don't want to create "hills" or "valleys" in the surface of the axe. With a belt sander, this is easier to avoid since you have a large, flat plane that you're essentially laying on the cheek of the axe.

Restore the Poll

Once you've cleaned up the surface of the axe, you can then restore the poll to its original form. If the axe was ever used as a hammer, the poll will need some light grinding to remove burrs and mushroomed edges. With the axe laid flat in the vise, make long, smooth strokes to clean up the mushroomed poll. You may also find that the top edge of the axe needs light grinding

How Much Hardened Steel Is Left?

We think of the axe as a single piece of metal, but in reality it's made of two very different metals. The cheek and eye are all made of relatively soft steel that can absorb the impact associated with chopping. The bit of the axe (and in some cases the poll) is made from much harder heat-treated steel that has been tempered to hold an edge. If you're buying a rusty old axe, you may not be able to tell if the treated steel has been ground away by just looking at it. One way to know for sure is to soak it in a vinegar bath for 24 hours. Not only will this clean off the rust, it will also reveal the "hamon line" which is the point at which the tempered and untreated steel intersect. This line is created by controlled cooling during the hardening/tempering process. This will visually tell you how much good steel you have left on your axe.

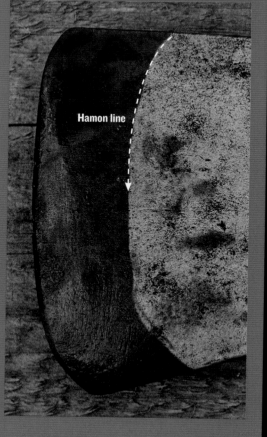

Hamon line

as well; this is often the result of using a hammer, instead of a wood or rubber mallet, to drive out an old handle. Go slowly and remove as little metal as possible.

Crafting a Keen Edge

Ask two woodsmen how to sharpen an axe, and you're liable to get three answers. Some swear by a filed edge, while others believe in only using a whetstone. Still others use bench grinders or belt sanders. My experience is that the condition of the bit and the quality of the steel are the two factors that determine which tool I use for sharpening.

Keep in mind that through use and abuse, the geometry of the axe changes as the bit is worn back, creating a thicker edge more suitable to splitting than chopping. Importantly, felling axes shouldn't be filed sharp; a blunt, thick edge is more durable and will resist chipping.

Sharpening with a belt grinder. If the bit of your axe has chips, gouges, and other imperfections, use the belt-grinder method outlined in this section. Do not use an angle grinder for sharpening the edge of your axe. The wheel of an angle grinder is too small to create a smooth, even bit; you'll end up with a bit that is thick in some places and thin in others. What's more, the heat created by grinders can result in hot spots that ruin the temper, or hardness of the axe. A more effective tool for sharpening dull and damaged axes is a narrow-gauge belt sander (1⅛ inches × 21 inches).

To begin, use 180-grit sandpaper belts. Before you even plug the sander in, practice drawing the sander back and forth, following the radius of the axe. The sander should point toward the poll of the axe as you do this, and be angled upward at approximately 20 to 25 degrees. Once you're comfortable

with the motion, you can begin grinding by using light strokes. Be sure to count the number of strokes so that you maintain an even bit angle on both sides. Check the bit regularly; if it's too hot to touch, you're either going too fast or applying too much pressure. As you flip the axe from side to side, use a small piece of hardwood to drive off the metal burr that forms as the bit of the axe is thinned to an apex. If you don't, you'll end up with a brittle wire edge that will break off. Once you've removed the major imperfections in the axe, switch to 220-grit sandpaper belts. When the bit is free of nicks and imperfections, you're ready to hone with a whetstone.

Sharpening with a bastard file. An alternative to the belt-sander method is the single-cut bastard file. I prefer this method for axes that have soft steel or only minor dings that need to be removed. The file can be used freehand or with a jig.

The jig maintains a constant 20-degree angle at all times.

Honing with a Whetstone

The last step in sharpening the axe is to use a whetstone on the actual cutting edge. This final cutting edge is about 10 degrees stouter than the grinding or filing angle. You can use either a hard Arkansas stone or a long-lasting but expensive diamond stone. As with grinding and filing, it is important to maintain a constant angle; for that reason, I prefer long, even strokes over small, circular strokes. Be sure to do an equal number of strokes on each side and, as in the grinding process, drive off the burr with a piece of clean hardwood. A sharp axe will be able to shave the hair on your arm or cleanly slice a sheet of paper. Like most other skills, sharpening an axe with finesse takes time and patience, but the investment pays dividends in the woodlot.

Sharpening with a bastard file

Honing with a whetstone

Naming Your Axe

The tradition of naming axes can be traced to the Vikings, and who could blame them as these weapons and tools were inextricably tied to their survival. Names inspired by Norse mythology — Freya, Sloveig, Ivar, and Oden — all top the list. Lumberjacks also named their axes, in many cases after the women they missed!

An unofficial poll of Axe Junkies turned up the following "common" axe names:

- Albatross
- Elvira
- Elvis
- Bertha
- Swiss Miss

- Precious
- Carvy
- Perfect
- The Destroyer
- The Persuader

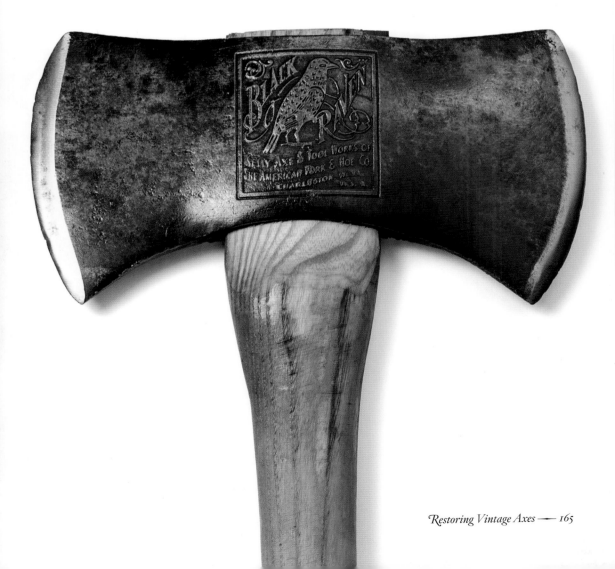

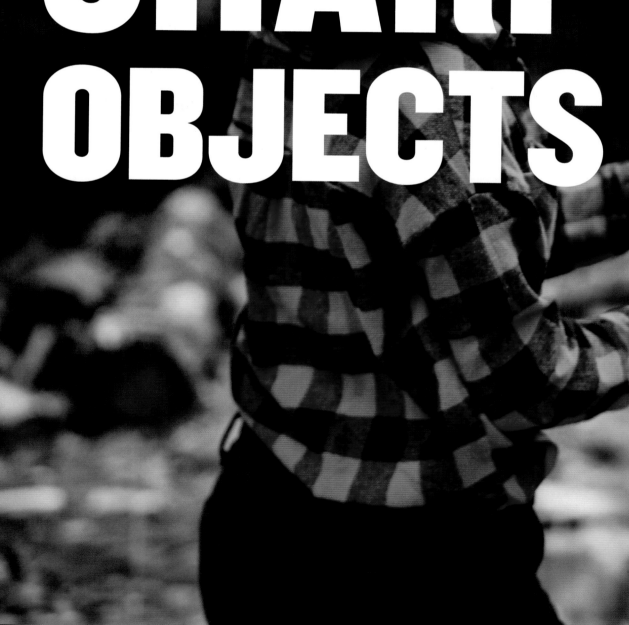

CHAPTER 6

PLAYING WITH SHARP OBJECTS

A LTHOUGH AXES ARE AMONG THE
MOST SERIOUS OF TOOLS, THEY CAN
ALSO BE A HECK OF A LOT OF FUN!
By taking a few safety precautions (and
leaving the beer 'til the end), you'll enjoy the
wide world of axe sports. If backyard bocce is
a bit tame for your tastes, maybe it's time for
some backyard tomahawk and axe throwing.
Or how about a round of lumberjack whac-
a-mole? Your summer barbecue will never be
the same again.

Axe Throwing

WHY THROW AN AXE, you ask? Because you can! Throwing a 3½-pound axe from 20 feet and sticking it in a bull's-eye the size of a hockey puck is downright exhilarating. In time you'll develop the feel of the axe and know if you're going to hit your target while the axe is still midair. The following tips apply whether you're throwing at an official axe-throwing venue or in your own backyard.

Throwing Safely

Let's start with one simple, but important, ground rule: never throw an axe or tomahawk if there are people or pets standing in front of, beside, or behind the target. Makes sense, right?

The throwing zone. One common misconception is that smaller axes or tomahawks can be thrown in a smaller area. But because they're lighter, they often ricochet for quite a distance, so they require the same amount of space a full-size throwing axe does: a 40-foot × 60-foot area. This creates a 20-foot deflection zone on each side of the target and a 40-foot overthrow area. Risk beyond the target can be reduced by creating a large plywood backstop, or by situating the target in front of a dense patch of trees.

At axe-throwing venues and bars, the throwing zone is typically a 4 foot × 20 foot × 10 foot cage that provides coverage on all sides, including the top. If you become passionate about throwing but only have a small backyard in a densely populated area, you could certainly build one out of chain link!

A tight head and a dull blade. All throwing tomahawks and axes need to be pinned. This is accomplished by drilling a hole through the eye of the axe (including the handle) and inserting a spring roll pin that extends from one side of the eye to the other. The idea is that if the head were to loosen while throwing, you'd still have a pin binding the head and handle together. Unpinned throwing axes have injured both throwers and bystanders.

Finally, I get a lot of questions asking how sharp a throwing axe or tomahawk should be. The answer is: it shouldn't be sharp at all. A sharp throwing axe simply adds danger to an already dangerous activity and increases the chances of chipping or damaging the bit. The goal of axe throwing isn't to cut anything, it's simply to wedge the axe in the target.

20' overthrow area at each side of target

40' overthrow area behind target

20' throwing distance

Axe-Throw Tic-Tac-Toe

For those who have a bit more space available for axe games (and multiple throwing axes with different colored handles for each player), consider Axe-Throw Tic-Tac-Toe. The tic-tac-toe board consists of nine stump cross sections (which can be smaller than a standard target) fashioned to a an 8-foot × 8-foot backstop of ⅜-inch CDX plywood mounted on 4×4 posts. The cross sections are lag-screwed from the back of the wall. The game is then played in standard tic-tack-toe format, alternating between players. If an axe misses the target, it can be retrieved and used on the next turn.

The Target

A backyard target can be constructed from a large cross-section of a tree trunk — ideally, 20 inches in diameter and 8 to 12 inches thick. Softwoods (such as pine or balsam) are preferable; the axe sticks more easily. If the cross section has knots, the knottiest side should become the backside of the target. The face of the target should have concentric circles every four inches from the center of the cross-section, with alternating paint colors.

The target should be mounted with 6-inch lag screws to a sturdy A-frame stand constructed of 2×6 lumber. The legs should be approximately 3 feet apart and measure 5 feet from the center of the target to the base of the legs. The end of each leg should be staked in the ground.

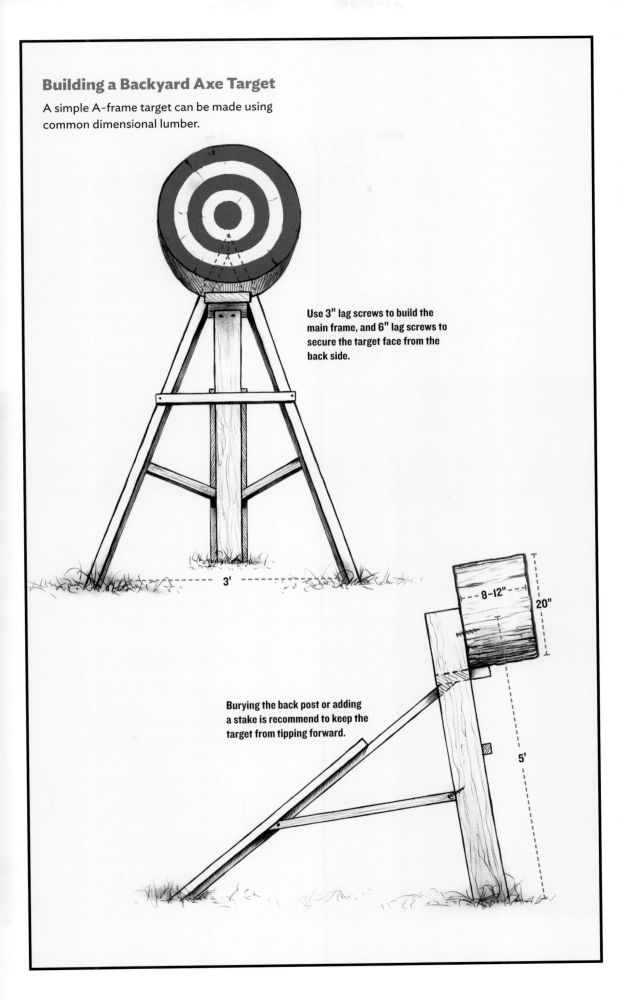

Building a Backyard Axe Target

A simple A-frame target can be made using common dimensional lumber.

Use 3" lag screws to build the main frame, and 6" lag screws to secure the target face from the back side.

Burying the back post or adding a stake is recommend to keep the target from tipping forward.

3'

8–12"

20"

5'

Selecting and Throwing an Axe

ONE COMMON MISCONCEPTION is that an axe is harder to throw than a tomahawk. The reality is that the mass of an axe is actually helpful in developing precision and repeatability. For those who find a 3½-pound axe too heavy, there are lighter models that have all the same dimensions as the larger axes, but are made of an aluminum alloy. A competition-quality axe will have a handle that's at least 24 inches long, a bit that's less than 6 inches wide, and a head that is pinned to the handle.

The Rules of Axe Throwing

✱ The regulation throwing distance is 20 feet, and the thrower may not cross the line before sticking the axe in the target.

✱ Each thrower is given one warm-up throw and three competition throws.

✱ The center of the bull's-eye is placed 5 feet above the ground.

✱ The bull's-eye is worth 5 points. Subsequent rings are worth 4, 3, 2, and 1.

✱ If the axe "double-sticks" (with both bits sticking in the target), the thrower is allowed to tap the axe handle. If the axe remains in the target for at least 5 seconds, the thrower is awarded the points corresponding with the leading edge.

✱ In the event of a tie between two throwers, each thrower is given one additional throw. The competitor who is closest to the center of the bull's-eye wins.

A Rowdy Good Time

Just as the rodeo evolved from ranching, lumberjack sports evolved from the work that made up the livelihood of loggers. The one exception to that might be axe throwing. Accounts from logging camps indicate that axe throwing was both a form of entertainment and a way to decide who did the undesirable camp tasks such as cleaning the outhouse. Today competitive lumberjacks throw axes for prize money, as well as a few competitions that replace the bull's-eye of the target with a hole that's just large enough to hold a can of soda. Hit the bull's-eye, and you'll be running to the target with your mouth agape in order to enjoy the cascading soda.

Axe-Throwing Technique

Although a variety of techniques exist, this is the method that I teach to collegiate lumberjacks. Hand and foot placement is described for right-handers; reverse the feet and hands for lefties.

Step to the throwing line 20 feet from the face of the target. Place your left foot in line with the bull's-eye. ▶

Hold the axe in your right hand about 5 inches from the end of the axe with your thumb pointed upwards. ▶

Swing the axe at your right side, then bring the axe up over your head and add your left hand below your right hand. Your left thumb should also be pointed up to prevent the axe from over-rotating. ▶

With the axe centered above your head, bring it back to the 10 o'clock position. (Any farther, and you'll risk scraping or cutting your back.) ▶

178

Bring the axe forward and release it as you feel the weight of the axe transition from behind your head to in front of you. Follow through with your throw, hands pointed at the bull's-eye. ■

Selecting and Throwing a Tomahawk

Ever since those glorious days of my boyhood in Kentucky it has seemed to me that throwing the tomahawk should be one of the regular feats at all American athletic meets.
— Daniel Beard, 1909

Throwing tomahawks tend to be more widely available and less expensive than throwing axes, and there are several dozen types. In addition to traditional tomahawks, there are modern one-piece tomahawks that remove the danger of the axe head and handle separating. Tomahawk throwing is governed by the American Knife Throwers Alliance (AKTA) which stipulates that tomahawks should have a minimum handle length of 12 inches from bottom of handle to the top of handle and the maximum cutting bit should be no more than 4½ inches along the curve of the blade.

The Rules of Tomahawk Throwing

Instead of a single target, as is commonly used in axe throwing, many tomahawk competitions use five targets arranged in a box pattern, with one center target that can be used for practice.

- The throwing distance is 13 feet and you may not step over the line.
- A total of four tomahawks are thrown at the outer four targets (leaving the center target unused).
- The bull's-eye on the target is worth 5 points; subsequent rings are worth 4 and 3 points.
- This is done five times for a total of 20 hawks, for a possible total point score of 100 points.
- Alternatively, some tomahawk competitions have adopted the single-target, three-throw rules that govern axe throwing.

Tomahawk-Throwing Technique

Hand and foot placement is described for right-handers; reverse feet and hands for lefties.

Step to the throwing line 13 feet from the face of the target. Place your left foot in line with the bull's-eye. ▶

Hold the tomahawk in your right hand and grip it like you would a hammer. If you discover that the tomahawk over-rotates, you can point your thumb up on the handle. ▼

Swing the tomahawk at your right side, then bring it back over your shoulder. ▶

As your tomahawk passes the side of your head, release it as if you were throwing a baseball. ▼

Follow through with your throw, hand pointed at the bull's-eye. ◾

Other Lumberjack Games

The watermelon challenge. This is an event that dates to early New England harvest fairs. In the fall before the lumberjacks returned to the forest for a winter of cutting wood, they'd attend the local fair for the watermelon challenge. A series of 30-foot poles were lined up and each lumberjack was given a watermelon to place four paces in front of their pole, before they started chopping. Whoever's pole smashed the watermelon first won the competition. Once all the lumberjacks were done, the spectators were invited onto the field for smashed watermelon.

Lumberjack stump. For those of a certain age or inclination, you may remember a game from college called "nails" or "stump." In the original version of stump, you sat around a log with protruding nails and took one swing per turn trying to drive the nail into the block. The winner was the person who could drive it flush in the least number of swings.

The lumberjack version is a test of accuracy and brute strength. It features a stump with a uniform dot spray painted in the center of it, and the goal is to split the stump into a total of four pieces with paint on them, in as few swings as possible.

Lumberjack whac-a-mole. This iteration of the classic game involves two competitors racing to split his/her large cross section of a log into firewood, using a splitting axe or maul, and shoving all the pieces into a 6-inch-round hole in the top of a plastic barrel. If a piece gets stuck in the top of the barrel, the competitor can only use other pieces of firewood to whack it through the hole. The first competitor to get all their pieces into the barrel wins!

Index

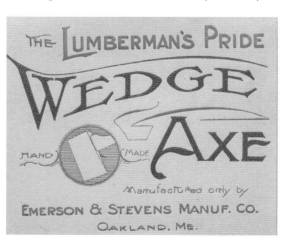

THE LUMBERMAN'S PRIDE
WEDGE AXE
HAND MADE
Manufactured only by
EMERSON & STEVENS MANUF. CO.
OAKLAND. ME.

ACKNOWLEDGMENTS

In the age of digital everything, analog people with their anachronistic skills are the folks I want in my tribe. These are the people who get excited by rusty metal, and the prospect of making old, forgotten things new and relevant. The irony that I met many of these folks via social media isn't lost on me. Instead, I'm grateful that there are platforms that allow us to connect, share our collective knowledge, and swap axes. At the top of that list would be the Axe Junkies and the nearly 40,000 members that make up this group, as well as many affiliate groups. This book wouldn't have been possible without the assistance of these members who vetted historical accounts, offered advice, and provided axe ephemera for the book. I'd also like to thank Craig Roost, head Axe Junkie and Council Tool Axe Designer, for supplying both axes and anecdotes. A huge thanks goes to Mark Ferguson and the Brant & Cochran team in Portland, Maine, who allowed us to take over their forge and factory for many of the photos in this book. The Six Nations Indian Museum in Onchiota, New York, provided the original stone and early trade tomahawks featured in the book. I'd also like to thank the members of the Paul Smith's College Woodsmen's Team who were happy to (safely) play with axes and demonstrate their proper use. Finally, I'd like to thank my wife, Carleen, for understanding that the hundreds of axes I've collected are all important research objects that contributed to this book, not some sort of sick obsession, or hobby gone off the rails . . . I swear.

THE
AROOSTOOK AXE
WEDGE

MANUFACTURED BY

Emerson & Stevens Man'f'g Co.

THE

LEWSEN SPECIAL

(Not Warranted)

Your money refunded if this is not the best axe you ever purchased at this price.

Manufactured by

MARSH & SONS CO.